T0343926

The censor's new clothes

EDITORIAL

45(04): 1/3 | DOI: 10.1177/0306422016685961

by **Rachael Jolley**

Governments introduce bans on clothing and other forms of expression are sending a signal about their own lack of confidence

IF YOU HAVE to introduce laws telling your citizens that they are banned from wearing purple, sporting red velvet, or showing their knees, then, frankly, you are in trouble.

But again and again, when times get tough or leaders think they should be, governments tell their people what to wear, or more often, what not to wear.

"Dare to wear this," they say, "and we will be down on you like a ton of bricks." Why any government thinks this is going to improve their power, the economy or put their country on a better footing is a mystery. History suggests you never strike up a more profitable relationship with your people by removing the freedom to wear specific types of clothing or, conversely, telling everyone that they have to wear the same thing. We are either consumed by rebellion, or by dullness.

The Romans tried it with purple (only allowed for the emperor and his special friends). The Puritans tried it with gold and silver (just for the magistrates and a few highfaluting types). Right now the governments of Saudi Arabia and Iran ban women from wearing anything but head-to-toe cover-ups along with a range of other limitations. In one frightening case in the past month there were calls via social media for a woman in Saudi Arabia to be killed because she went out shopping "uncovered" without a *hijab* or *abaya*. One tweet read: "Kill her and throw her corpse to the dogs."

Banning any type of freedom of expression, often including free speech, or freedom of assembly, usually happens in times of national angst, economic downturn or crisis, when governments are not acting either in the interest of their people, or the national good. These are not healthy, confident nations, but nations that fear allowing their people to speak, act and think. And that fear can express itself in mandating or restricting types of expression. Generally, as with other restrictions on freedom found in the US First Amendment, enforcing such bans doesn't sweep in a period of prosperity for countries that impose them.

At different points in world history governments have forced a small group of people to wear particular things, or tried to wipe out styles of clothing they did not approve of. In medieval Europe, for instance, non-Christians were, at certain periods, forced to wear badges such as stars or crescents as were Christians who refused to conform to a state religion, such as the Cathars. Forcing a particular badge or clothing to be worn sends a signal of exclusion. Those →

ABOVE: Protesters demonstrate against France's ban of the burkini, outside the French Embassy in London

→ authorities are, by implication, saying to the majority that there is a difference in the status of the minority, and in doing so opening them up either to attack, or at least suspicion. Not much has changed between then and now. Historically groups that have been forced to wear some kind of badge or special outfit have then found themselves ostracised or physically attacked. The most obvious modern example is Jews being forced to wear yellow stars in Nazi Germany, but this is not the only time minorities have been legally forced to stand out from the crowd. In 2001 the Taliban ruled that Afghan Hindus had to wear a public label to signify they were non-Muslims. The intent of such actions are clear: to create tension.

The other side of this clothing coin is when clans, tribes or groups who choose to dress differently from the mainstream, for historical religious reasons, or even just because they follow a particular musical style, are persecuted because of that visual difference, because of what it stands for, or because they are seen as rebelling against

authority. In some cases strict laws have been put in place to try and force change, in other cases certain people decide to take action. In 1746, for instance, the British government banned kilts and tartans (except for the military) under the Dress Act, a reaction said to be motivated by support for rebellions to return Catholic (Stuart) monarchs to the British throne. Those who ignored the order faced six months in prison for the first instance, and seven years deportation for the second. Those who wear distinctive, and traditional clothing, out of choice can face other disadvantages. For years, the Oromo people in Ethiopia, who wear distinctive clothing, have long faced discrimination, but in 2016 dozens of Oromo people were killed at a religious festival, after police fired bullets into the crowd (see page 32). And in her article Eliza Vitri Handayani reports on how the punk movement in Indonesia has attracted animosity and in one case, Indonesian police seized 64 punks, shaved their heads and forced them to bathe in a river to "purify themselves". Recently the Demak branch of

Nadhlatul Ulama, Indonesia's largest Islamic organisation, has banned reggae and punk concerts because they make young people "dress weird" .

Another cover for restrictions or bans stems from religions. As soon as the word "modesty" is bandied around as a reason for somebody to be prohibited from wearing something then you know you have to worry. Strangely, it is never the person who proclaims that there needs to be a bit more modesty who needs to change their ways. Of course not. It is other people who need to get a lot more modest. The inclusion of modesty standards tends to be used to get women to cover up more than they have done.

Then you get officious types who decide that they have the measure of morality, and start hitting women wearing short skirts (as is happening right now in South Africa and Uganda). For some Ugandan women it feels like a return to the 1970s under dictator Idi Amin "morality" laws.

Trans people can find themselves confronting laws, sometimes centuries old, that lay out what people shouldn't be allowed to wear. In Guyana a case continues to edge through the court of appeal this year, it argues that a cross-dressing law from 1893 allows the police to arrest or harass trans people. A new collection, the Museum of Transology, which opens in London in January, uses a crowdsourced collection of objects and clothing to chart modern trans life and its conflicts with the mainstream, from a first bra to binders.

When freedom of expression is quashed, it usually finds a way of squeezing out just to show that the spirit is not vanquished. So during the tartan ban in the 18th century, there are tales of highlanders hiding a piece of tartan under other clothes to have it blessed at a Sunday service. And certainly tartan and plaids are plentiful in Scotland today. In the 1930s and 40s when British women and girls were not "expected" to wear trousers or shorts, some bright spark designed a split

skirt that could be worn for playing sport. It looked like a short dress (therefore conforming to the accepted code), but they were split like shorts allowing girls to run around with some freedom.

While in Iran, where rules about "modest" dress are enforced viciously with beatings, sales of glitzy high heels go through the roof. No one can stop those women showing the world their personal style in any way they can. Iranian model and designer Tala Raassi, who grew up in Iran, has written about how vital those signs of style are to Iranian women. In a recent article, commenting on the recent burkini ban in France, Raassi wrote of her disappointment that a democratic country would force an individual to put on or take of a piece of clothing. She added: "Freedom is not about the amount of

When freedom of expression is quashed, it usually finds a way of squeezing out just to show that the spirit is not vanquished

clothing you put on or take off, but about having the choice to do so."

And that freedom is the clearest sign of a healthy country. We must support the freedom for individuals to make choices, even if we do not agree with them personally. The freedom to be different, if one chooses to be, must not be punished by some kind of lower status or ostracism. National leaders have to learn that taking away freedom of expression from their people is a sign of their failure. Countries with the most freedom are the ones that will historically be seen as the most successful politically, economically and culturally. ⊗

Rachael Jolley is the editor of Index on Censorship magazine. She recently won the editor of the year (special interest) at British Society of Magazine Editors' 2016 awards

CONTENTS

INDEX ON CENSORSHIP
VOLUME 45 NUMBER 04 – WINTER 2016

BRITISH SOCIETY OF MAGAZINE EDITORS AWARDS 2016 WINNER

EDITOR
Rachael Jolley
DEPUTY EDITORS
Vicky Baker, Sally Gimson, Georgia Hussey
SUB EDITORS
Alex Dudok de Wit, Jan Fox
CONTRIBUTING EDITORS:
Irene Caselli (Argentina), Jan Fox (US), Kaya Genç (Turkey), Natasha Joseph (South Africa), Jemimah Steinfeld

EDITORIAL ASSISTANT
Kieran Etoria-King
DESIGN
Matthew Hasteley
COVER
Ben Jennings
THANKS TO:
Jodie Ginsberg, Sean Gallagher, Ryan McChrystal

Magazine printed by Page Bros., Norwich, UK

Index on Censorship | +44 (0) 20 7963 7262
292 Vauxhall Bridge Road, London SW1V 1AE, United Kingdom

Supported by
ARTS COUNCIL ENGLAND

MODEL: Melodie

SPECIAL REPORT

FASHION RULES, DRESSING TO OPPRESS: WHY DRESS CODES AND FREEDOM CLASH

MODELS: Lola, Melodie, Tiger-Lily, Amina

CREDIT: Loanna Hoffmann/Foto24/Gallo

Fashion police

45(04): 10/13 | DOI: 10.1177/0306422016685962

Ugandan and South African women who wear miniskirts are facing attacks from private citizens. **Natasha Joseph** speaks to some of the women who are challenging what is happening

AS FAR AS the man groping her in broad daylight in the middle of Uganda's capital city was concerned, Patience Akumu was the one breaking the law. After all, she was dressed "indecently", in a dress that fell slightly above her knee and which revealed her shoulders. And that was a contravention of the African nation's newly tabled Anti-Pornography Act. The act, according to an article in the local Daily Monitor

Speaking to Index on Censorship from Kampala, Akumu said that "on paper", Ugandan women's freedom of expression is protected. It's enshrined in the country's constitution, despite its growing reputation as a nation of fundamentalist Christians, Uganda is secular.

The attempt to control women's dress is a return to the 1970s when the country's leader, dictator Idi Amin, banned women from wearing trousers, revealing dresses, long skirts with splits as well as miniskirts and hotpants. Many girls and young women were fined by magistrates and a few even given jail sentences. Amin himself though was famously photographed with model, politician and lawyer Princess Elizabeth Bagaya of Toro who wore shorts for the occasion.

LEFT: Women in Johannesburg, South Africa, protest against the harassment of women who wear miniskirts

Private citizens rather than the state have taken it upon themselves to play the role of guardians of the country's moral order

newspaper, outlawed "anything that shows sexual parts of a person such as breasts, thighs, buttocks or any erotic behaviour intended to cause sexual excitement or any indecent act or behaviour tending to corrupt morals, among other things".

Supposedly, the act was going to make Uganda's women safer. Instead, as Akumu discovered in Kampala on that day in 2014, it spurred on a section of the population which believed women shouldn't be allowed to wear what they choose.

Akumu is a human rights activist, writer and feminist. Her experience drove her and a group of human rights advocates to organise a demonstration against the controversial piece of legislation. She also set up a Facebook page, End Miniskirt Harassment, to give women a platform.

Despite Amin's rules, Ugandan women didn't come to physical harm if they violated the laws. Even in "up-country" rural areas, which tend to be more traditional and staid, said Akumu, women weren't attacked for wearing supposedly revealing clothing. The attitude from men and elders "was never outright; it was quite subtle. You wouldn't be beaten up, but there would be disapproval."

Then came 2014 and things started to change. In the run up to the national elections in February 2016, politicians tabled a wave of "morality" laws. They included the internationally reviled Anti-Homosexuality Act, which would later be overturned. The Anti-Pornography Act was also tabled at this time. Akumu said its "ambiguous" definitions of "pornography" and "exposure" were problematic. And although it didn't →

→ mention miniskirts or women's clothing choices, the act gave voice to those who wanted women to cover up.

These voices had a powerful ally in the form of Uganda's rather grandly named state minister for ethics and integrity, whose department is housed in the office of the presidency. Minister Simon Lokodo is no fan of the miniskirt. He had pushed for some time to have these supposedly offensive garments banned in Uganda, explaining in 2013: "Any attire which exposes intimate parts of the human body, especially areas that are of erotic function, is outlawed. Anything above the knee is outlawed. If a woman wears a miniskirt we will arrest her." At another stage, he suggested that women who displayed their legs were dangerous. They distracted male drivers for one thing.

Akumu said that before the act had even been passed by Uganda's parliament, vigilante groups began roaming the country stripping women they claimed were "obscenely" dressed.

After her own harrowing encounter with a man who claimed she deserved to be groped since her knees and shoulders were visible, Akumu decided to organise a demonstration

There is something about Johannesburg that belongs to men. Women are always interlopers, they don't really belong

opposing the act. She struggled to get police clearance for the gathering, telling the BBC that she'd been turned away from several police stations because officers complained she wasn't appropriately dressed. In the end, the protest went ahead. It was attended by 200 people and, Akumu said, put pressure on the police to start taking vigilante attacks on "obscenely dressed" women a bit more seriously. Some men were arrested. Others

continued to verbally hound women, telling them: "I see how you're dressed, but I know I can't do anything. I'll be arrested."

Sadly, the attacks persist. Akumu told Index that lobbying around the issue was tough: "When it comes to women and freedom of expression, and them dressing in a way that people consider 'inappropriate', there's little interest or action." She contrasted this with widespread global condemnation of the Anti-Homosexuality Act, which created so much pressure that President Yoweri Museveni decided not to challenge a constitutional court ruling that overturned the legislation.

Akumu said that even many feminist activists in Uganda preferred to focus on what they perceived as more important issues, such as female genital mutilation and the need to improve girls' schooling. And ordinary Ugandans, she said, sometimes seemed to think that "women should be grateful for the rights they have".

"There's almost a sense that while women should have their rights, there's a limit, a ceiling to these rights," she said.

For Akumu and her peers in Uganda, the battle continues. But theirs is far from the only African nation that believes it's acceptable to control women's clothing choices. Kenyan journalist Samantha Spooner told Index she felt far less comfortable wearing shorts or a skirt in Nairobi than she would elsewhere.

"In general this is a patriarchal society, though more and more women are getting appointed into higher positions. This doesn't however dilute the elements of discrimination you'll face or see as a woman, like male-dominated panels in conferences, being consistently spoken over in a conversation, expected not to air your opinions in a meeting or to accept when a man pushes in front of you in a queue," Spooner said. "Just to show how much men can get away with, in 2013 the Nairobi governor Evans Kidero slapped the women's representative Rachel

Shebesh outside his office. It was caught on film but he kept his job."

This sense of impunity extends to policing women's clothing choices – and has done for a long time in Kenya, Uganda and across most of the rest of Africa. South African professor Louise Vincent has researched the history of women being targeted for "daring" to dress in a way that men think is inappropriate or doesn't conform to their ideas of femininity. In an article titled Women's Rights Get A Dressing Down: Miniskirt Attacks in South Africa, Vincent wrote: "Controversy over the clothing choices of African women is not new. In the immediate postcolonial period African leaders across the continent took a personal interest in what women wore and berated them for 'unsuitable' choices."

In some cases, Vincent pointed out, these women's choices of "modern" clothing that was popular in the West were linked to colonialism, a system the continent was trying to cast off once and for all after centuries of control and invasion.

"Miniskirts in particular became, for many African leaders, emblematic of both the continued intrusion of colonial ideas despite formal liberation and of the moral degeneration, particularly of urban black youth, as a result of this intrusion," Vincent wrote.

The major shift since then, in South Africa particularly, has been that private citizens rather than the state have "taken it upon themselves to play the role of guardians of the country's moral order". Men frequently police women's behaviour, often violently. South African theatre director Clara Vaughan created the play Noord! because she'd read a story about two women who were attacked, groped and taunted by a mob of men while at one of Johannesburg's biggest commuter taxi ranks, Noord. It wasn't the first attack of its kind at the rank, but because it was captured on video this incident became a massive national talking point.

Vaughan said these kinds of attacks on women in public places stemmed from men having "a sense of ownership, both of public space and women's bodies".

"It's particularly striking to me that Johannesburg, even more than other cities, is such a historically masculine space. Men migrating or immigrating here to look for work on the mines, living in hostels, and so

Miniskirts became, for many African leaders, emblematic of both colonialism and moral degeneration

on. There is something about the identity of the city that belongs to men. So women are always interlopers, they don't really belong.

"And so they can be challenged and policed. Women who give the impression of being in control of, or enjoying, their sexuality are particularly threatening to men who think female sexuality should be controlled by men. That's why I think women in 'sexy' clothing are so often the victims of assault. Black women, in particular, are under extraordinary pressure to conform to the 'correct' model of femininity, the correct combination of tradition and modernity, sexiness and modesty, and so on."

The freedom to wear what you choose is also an indicator of how free a society is, and its attitudes to the equality of its citizens. In some parts of Africa all the gains made for women risk being set back if countries' laws and cultural mores continue to dictate what should or shouldn't be worn. These laws are not just about clothing, but are a sign of something greater. ⊗

Natasha Joseph is a contributing editor for Index on Censorship magazine, based in Johannesburg, South Africa. She is also Africa education, science and technology editor at The Conversation

Wearing a T-shirt got me arrested

45(04): 14/17 | DOI: 10.1177/0306422016685968

Former editor of Elle magazine **Maggie Alderson** remembers how she was hauled in front of magistrates for wearing punk clothes and argues that British young people can now dress how they like

WHEN I WAS a teenage punk rocker, 40 years ago, you could get beaten up on the streets of Britain just for wearing skinny jeans. Your assailants might be Teddy Boys, wearing the narrowest of trousers themselves, furious at your audacity for encroaching on their tribal style domain. Or skinheads in classic Levi's, hoisted calf-high by braces, who hated you just for existing.

I managed to escape the aggressors – I was little and nippy – many of my friends didn't, but it wasn't just thugs who were on our case for how we dressed, as I discovered when I was arrested on London's Clapham High Street, thrown into a police car and charged with obscenity, and later hauled up in front of lay judges at Lavender Hill Magistrates Court, just for wearing a particular T-shirt.

The garment in question was from designer Vivienne Westwood's shop Seditionaries and featured an illustration by Tom of Finland (a mid-20th century gay artist) featuring two untrousered and marvellously well-endowed cowboys, chatting. I still have it.

That was what you risked for sartorially expressing your identity as a punk rocker, but even regular citizens were subject to stringent and limiting dress codes. Women over the age of 40 were expected to dress in a way which was "age appropriate" (dull) and even post-1960s flower power, men could put themselves at risk of jeers, or even a beating, by wearing colours deemed "effeminate". You didn't see any pink shirts in the City of London then. Now, it's awash with them.

Even beyond conventions, repression and social mores, there was another major restriction on most people expressing themselves creatively through fashion. Money. If you couldn't afford to shop in the luxury department store Harrods, or on Bond Street, where designers still have their boutiques, there really wasn't much fashion to buy. There were clothes for the masses – but not high fashion, the latest ideas and styles. That was an elite pursuit.

The few chain stores in existence were dismal places – as anyone who can remember the communal changing rooms of the high street shop Miss Selfridge will tell you. If you weren't having your handbag nicked, you were being asphyxiated by the smell of other people's feet, all in pursuit of poorly made clothing, in limited styles and horrible fabrics.

Basia Szkutnicka, formerly a lecturer at the London College of Fashion, and shortly

to become professor of fashion design at Hong Kong Polytechnic University, remembers what it was like when she was a student at St Martins School of Art in the mid-1980s.

"We didn't have Primark, a shop you could go to and get five pairs of socks for a £1. We had to shop at jumble sales and in charity shops, buy stuff and customise it," she said.

Compare that with the British high street of today, bursting with shops where you can get brilliant versions of the latest looks from the Paris and Milan catwalks, within a couple of weeks of the fashion shows taking place – much cheaper (relatively) than it was in the

1970s and 1980s and great quality too.

Indeed, so good are these chain store "tributes" now, that some major fashion houses – Burberry and Tom Ford, to name but two – have started selling their new styles from the moment the fashion show is over, rather than waiting six months as they used to.

So, in terms of what you can wear without risk of physical attack or social exclusion and what you can buy very cheaply, people in the UK have never had it so good.

And yet, while we didn't have chain store high fashion in the early 1980s, we did have the ground-breaking →

ABOVE: A group of young punks in London during the 1980s

ABOVE: Three highly styled friends talk outside Afro Punk festival 2016 in Alexandra Palace, London

→ street-style magazine iD, which featured photographs of real people, recruited on the street and at nightclubs, with captions listing what they were wearing, where they got it and how much they'd paid for it. There was prestige in how little your outfit cost.

Compare that, says Szkutnicka, to current

We were pushing boundaries in every direction and trying things on whether it was to shock or make people stare, or shout things at us

British magazines, which aren't much more than shopping lists, bossily instructing readers what they "need" to buy, with articles seriously headlined: "12 things you must buy this autumn".

One I just found on Grazia's website promotes: "The Rise of The Affordable 'It' Bag

- The 21 Best Designer Bags Under £500". I took an average and it came to £480 a bag. Affordable?

Adding to this message of style through spending are the legions of covertly sponsored fashion bloggers and Instagrammers, whose every garment has been supplied free in return for a glowing online mention.

"I teach all over the world," said Szkutnicka. "And while young people in the UK probably have the most freedom for fashion self-expression, they don't feel free in financial terms. They genuinely believe you need to have a lot of money, to buy a lot of things. Magazines tell them to be consumers and they believe it."

Iain R Webb, professor of fashion and design at Kingston School of Art and former magazine fashion director, knows more about self-expression through fashion than most: he was one of the legendary Blitz kids, the supercool gang who congregated at a small London weekly club night in 1979, where entrance was allowed only according to the outlandish creativity of your get-up. Boy George, Stephen Jones, John Galliano and Spandau Ballet were some of the other regulars.

"Back in the Blitz days, we had nothing," said Webb. "So it meant we had nothing to lose by doing anything. We were pushing boundaries in every direction and trying things on whether it was to shock or make people stare, or shout things at us."

His own students, he is surprised and disturbed to find, increasingly don't feel so free to push the limits, not for fear of personal injury, but of causing offence to others.

Webb cites the outcry that happened in September, when US fashion designer Marc Jacobs had the models' hair styled in brightly coloured dreadlocks for his fashion show, which he says was inspired by the hairdo Webb's contemporary Boy George sported when he ascended to pop fame in the early 1980s. But the women on his catwalk were mostly white and Jacobs was accused of

cultural appropriation. He subsequently issued a formal apology.

"Where does that stop?" asked Webb. "That's a form of censorship. Kids in colleges are worrying about everything now – it limits what they feel they can do. Everything is tempered by 'I don't want to offend anybody…' when the whole point in art school is that you're pushing the boundaries, you want to be challenging and provoking.

"Self-censoring is not a good thing for any of the creative arts, which includes fashion."

So, four decades on from my experiences of being physically threatened and arrested for what I wore, British youth are now fully at liberty to express themselves through fashion, free from constraints of gender appropriateness and tribal dress codes, with a wealth of choice of affordable clothes on every high street.

Yet, within this new world of fashion freedom, new limiting factors have come to bear,

the difference being that they seem to come more from within than from outside forces. Could it be that creativity needs restriction to burgeon forth? And so where it no longer exists, the hive mind will contrive it. ⊗

Maggie Alderson is a former magazine editor for British Elle and fashion writer for The Times. She is also a bestselling novelist

---

SHORT HISTORY OF PUNK

1974: The term "punk rock" is first used to describe an underground scene in New York that includes bands such as The Ramones. Malcolm McLaren and Vivienne Westwood start the west London clothing boutique Sex, selling mainly rubber and fetish clothing. The store, through several iterations and renovations, would define the style of the punk subculture. The Sex Pistols begin to build a niche following in London.

1976: Anarchy in the UK is released, and The Sex Pistols, The Clash, The Damned and Johnny Thunders and the Heartbreakers unite for the Anarchy Tour. Several gigs are cancelled after sensationalist media reports of the behaviour of the bands and

their fans. The Nazi swastika emerges as a symbol of rebellion against the World War II generation, and many artists such as Sid Vicious wear it frequently.

1977: The iconic Roxy nightclub opens in Covent Garden, with a Sex Pistols concert on New Year's Day. In its first 100 days, the club hosts dozens of bands including The Damned, Buzzcocks, The Jam and The Police. Zandra Rhodes begins to introduce the trademark rips and safety pins of punk style into high fashion.

1979: The Specials release their debut album and Madness' One Step Beyond is a top 10 single, as punk's interaction with reggae and ska leads to the development of new genres and subcultures.

By Kieran Etoria-King

Colour bars

45(04): 18/20 | DOI: 10.1177/0306422016685969

Bright indigenous clothes in Bolivia help define social class. Writer **Magela Baudoin** says language is not changing with the times

IN BOLIVIA, THE South American country with the largest indigenous population, language is often used as a tool to insult, exclude and categorise according to the way they dress and their indigenous origins.

Pejorative terms such as *india*, *chola*, *birlocha* and *chota* are used to characterise women according to whether they are "pure" or "mixed race".

These terms are still commonly used, despite the political changes of the past 15 years, and the election of Evo Morales Ayma in 2006, the first indigenous president.

Definitions of these terms are prescriptively rigid. *India*, for instance, is used for a woman from the countryside who maintains "original" clothes and language.

Chola denotes a woman of mixed race and from the city, seen in the popular imagination as indigenous, typically dressed in the style of the colonial period, inspired by the dresses worn by Spanish women during the 17th century. The *chola* wear *pollera* – layered skirts, a *manta* – a shawl and a *sombrero borsalino* – a small bowler-style hat.

Next, *birlocha* means a woman who has abandoned the pollera to wear trousers, most often jeans, while simultaneously keeping her typical multi-coloured woven shawl, often used to strap an infant to her back, among other traditional features.

Meanwhile the *chota*, now detached from ethnicity, adopts lower middle-class western customs, wearing dresses that fit the body tightly.

Sociologist María Galindo, leader of the feminist movement Mujeres Creando (Creative Women), one of the main independent collectives in Bolivia, explained how these categories are applied to women, but not in the same way to men. She said: "There are numerous racist terms in daily use in our language, but the most common ones employed with reference to clothing would be: *chola*, *chota* and *birlocha*. These expressions are used as insults in everyday language, with a strong racist charge to them since all three are indicative of exclusion, of not belonging to the world of white women."

She added: "In addition, these insults demonstrate the strong constraints of social control over indigenous women's way of dressing, one that was never applied to indigenous men. While an indigenous man is able to move from wearing a poncho to a man's jacket or suit (often three-piece, a traditionally Western form of dress), without being pointed out or suffering humiliation, any indigenous woman who decides to wear a frock or a pair of trousers is exposed to ridicule and public scorn."

Political analyst and writer Fernando Molina said that in Bolivia, still a deeply conservative Catholic country, women are seen as playing certain roles according their place in the heavily stratified society. Different

CREDIT: Pablo Caridad / Alamy Stock Photo

tasks, he said, were assigned to "decent" whites, to *mestizos*, to *cholos* (those of mixed race), to indigenous people, as well as to men and women.

"Universal suffrage was only introduced into our country in 1952 and women were only fully included in the workplace during the 1970s. Land ownership according to legal franchise was reserved exclusively for men until 1996. Changes brought by modernity have been long delayed in Bolivia," he said.

However change is coming, and that means that Bolivian dress is being re-evaluated. Fashion is playing a large part in this.

The typical dress of the *chola* for instance has even been included, with a number of variations, on the international fashion circuit and at national, regional and local political level.

According to Molina: "The most likely thing is that it [the stratification] will disappear with time. Very few urban youths of indigenous origin decide to continue dressing like their mothers and grandmothers," he said.

He added: "There have never been instances of repression regarding the wearing of *chola* dress. Society coexists with it →

ABOVE: Bolivian women wearing traditional dresses on the day of Evo Morales' second presidential election

→ and, in certain cases respects and values it. The outfit is a cultural and political symbol, and you can see any number of extremely elegant variations of it glittering at popular fiestas. However, in everyday life, it is perceived as a sign of origin contributing to discrimination. This, and the fact that it can be uncomfortable to wear, explains its slow decline. "

Until the advent of Morales' presidency, it was at best difficult and often impossible for a woman dressed like a chola to go into a café or a restaurant

Numerous laws bringing more equality for women have been passed over the last 15 years: against racism, discrimination and violence, in support of sexual and reproductive rights; concerning identity and gender, quotas and political participation, amongst others.

However, the reality does not always keep up with the pace of legal reform. In 2015 Bolivia celebrated 34 years of democratic rule, and in those years female representation in the legislative assembly jumped from 2% to 52%, placing Bolivia second in the world for female political representation. But it is the Latin American country with the highest rate of violence against women, and the second, after Haiti, in sexual violence.

It was under Morales' government, one which has valued and recognised the symbolic value of indigenous origins, that a woman, a former domestic servant who wore a *pollera*, was made minister of justice, something inconceivable even at the end of the last century.

It is obvious that the political representation of indigenous communities has progressed. In effect many of them are or have been leaders and ministers of state.

According to Molina, however, although ethnic groups are more represented in public life, "racism, the nostalgia for a stratified society in which whites remain the privileged sector, persists surreptitiously and surfaces time and again in daily life, including road rage and types of insult."

Discrimination particularly against women is often tied to styles of dressing, because it is yet another way to censor, stereotype, separate out and establish hierarchies.

Until the advent of Morales' presidency, it was at best difficult and often impossible for a woman dressed like a *chola* to go into a café or a restaurant. It remains problematic, despite anti-discrimination legislation, to do so in places where the body is exposed, or in discos or elegant evening venues.

Galindo said that despite Morales presidency, there is still widespread discrimination. "There is a legitimate and glorious fury on the part of all underdogs, in favour of the destruction of a powerful white oligarchy that has governed our country since it was founded, and this strength pushed us to opt for a man such as Morales to be our president. His greatest political capital is his life story and skin colour. It is felt and lived in our daily lives. Nonetheless, from my point of view the institutional response remains too feeble and above all diminished. It remains trapped in folkloric gestures, symbolic acts lacking any real effect."

Much has changed. Our laws, the tolerance of racism, the unrestrained use of contemptuous language, the exclusivity of the white Western world and still one only has to scratch the surface a little with a fingernail and everything looks as if it has stayed just the same. The way ahead has far to go. ⊗

Translated by Amanda Hopkinson

Magela Baudoin *is a Bolivian writer and journalist, and winner of the Gabriel García Márquez short story prize 2015*

Models of freedom

45(04): 21/23 | DOI: 10.1177/0306422016685970

Designer **Bibi Russell** on how Bangladeshi women have growing economic power but are also facing restrictions on their freedom

I **GREW UP BEFORE** the independence of Bangladesh, when it was still East Pakistan. We lived in the old part of Dhaka, and my parents were very much part of the cultural and political scene here, so I was exposed to a mixed culture. We used to travel around Bangladesh a lot, to the villages, and people from the villages would also come to our home.

It was these village people and what they wore that has inspired me the most. I used to hear about Bangladesh being poor, but they would wear the most amazing clothes, beautifully hand-woven and colourful.

When I asked them where they got the clothes, they would say the weavers next door made them. My inspiration for fashion came from them. →

ABOVE: Garment workers wearing colourful fabrics in a clothing factory in Dhaka, Bangladesh

→ In some ways in my time there was much more freedom than today. You would be able to see the beautiful faces and bodies of women moving around. They would all be wearing saris.

The fashion landscape now in Bangladesh

The freedom in clothing women are now enjoying as they work is also clashing with another trend

is more complicated. In some ways working women are more independent and less hidden now. What is most striking about the Bangladesh fashion scene today is how colourful and brightly printed the clothes ordinary working women wear and how conspicuous they are. It is a big change over

the last 10 years, and a sign of women's growing sense of self-expression.

This has come about mainly because Bangladesh's economy depends on its female workforce. Women make up 80% of employees in the garment business, Bangladesh's largest industry. It accounts, according to World Bank figures, for 83% of total exports.

The growth of the clothing industry has given these women financial power and independence for the first time. A sense of this empowerment is shown in the clothes they wear and the fashion they have adopted.

In the past, Bengali women of all social backgrounds and status wore saris. Now, young women between the ages of 15 and 30 who are working or studying wear a *salwar kameez* (tunic and pyjamas) and a *dupatta* (scarf), as this is more comfortable and makes it easier to move freely to get to

|||||||||||||||||||||||||||||||||||||||||||||||||||||||||||||||||||||||||||||||||||||||||||

FROM MODEL TO DESIGNER

Bibi Russell was born in Chittagong and raised in Dhaka. Inspired by vibrant traditional clothing, she had an interest in fashion from a young age. In 1975 she fulfilled her dream of becoming the first Bangladeshi woman to graduate with a degree in fashion design at London School of Fashion. When she wore her own designs at her graduation show, she was approached by modelling agents, and soon appeared in international magazines such as Vogue, Harper's Bazaar and Cosmopolitan. She spent 20 years modelling all over the world for designers including Giorgio Armani, Karl Lagerfeld and Yves Saint-Laurent. When she returned to Bangladesh in 1994, she started visiting villages around the country for inspiration, before founding her clothing line Bibi Productions, aimed at making traditional fabrics more marketable. Her first European show, in Paris in 1996, brought work to 30,000 weavers in rural areas, according to UNESCO research. Russell develops handloom fabrics with colours that are non-chemically produced and environmentally friendly.

work or to school.

If you visit a garment factory or observe the lines of women walking down the street in Dhaka city, you will see girls in a myriad of bright colours: pinks, oranges, purples, greens, blues, with bright scarves covering their heads or draped over their chest, accessorised with shiny hair clips, earrings and bangles.

In the villages women are also wearing *salwar kameez* in public, and kaftans at home. There is variety in the fashion as well, with sleeve details of the tunics, and different kinds of *salwars*.

It was not always like this. In the 1980s and 1990s when women first came from the villages to the cities to work, the change in women's place in society was met with negativity by people who did not accept that women should out in public.

But a lot has changed since then and in the last decade NGOs and others have tirelessly advocated for women's empowerment and education, working for human rights and against sexual harassment.

The freedom in clothing women are now enjoying as they work is also clashing with another trend, and that is the increasing number of women who are choosing to wear the hijab. A lot of women in the cities and villages cover their hair and sometimes their faces with a *burqa* when in public.

But they don't always wear them for religious reasons. They wear them because they believe it protects them from rape, sexual harassment and acid burn attacks. There were 59 recorded acid attacks last year, according to the Bangladesh-based Acid Survivors Foundation.

The trend for wearing the *hijab* is an indication that the notion of freedom is ambiguous for women. It is both a symbol of subservience, and a provider of the feeling of protection and safety for women.

When I do my collections, especially abroad, I don't do traditional outfits, I do whatever I feel like at the time.

My biggest strength is the village people and the younger generation. Though they may be covering their bodies to feel more protected, this is also a way of making themselves more independent to move around in public. ⊗

Bibi Russell is a Bangladeshi fashion designer and former model

OPPOSITE: Bibi Russell (on right) greets the audience during Kolkata fashion week, surrounded by models wearing her fashion line

The big cover-up

45(04): 24/26 | DOI: 10.1177/0306422016685971

Laura Silvia Battaglia looks at the growing use of the abaya and niqab in Saudi Arabia and Yemen, and describes how women are giving these clothes their own stylistic twist

SARAH ATTAR, THE first female track athlete ever to represent Saudi Arabia at the Olympics, flew to Jeddah a year ago to meet the women members of the Jeddah Running Collective. "They're doing amazing things here," she tweeted. She met with Saudi women runners who run in an *abaya*, the traditional long black garment, mandatory for women in the Gulf state. Some runners even wear a *niqab*, the full veil that only shows the eyes. The women have been running since 2013 as a form of activism and protest, organising city runs with the hashtags #runinabaya, #doitinabaya and #bridgethegap. "I'd never run before and I felt a real need to do it," said runner Neshreen Gadesh. "I told myself: now go out and feel free."

The spread of the *abaya* and *niqab* in Saudi Arabia happened relatively recently, but its modern history can be traced back

CREDIT: Hani Mohammed/AP Photo

to 1932, when four distinct regions were united into a single state: modern-day Saudi Arabia. The new regime began to promote a branch of Sunnism that had been founded by the 18th-century preacher Muhammad ibn Abd al-Wahhab. Saudi Arabia's laws have been based on this creed's strict version of sharia law which incorporates desert traditions which have been taken into Islam. One of these customs is that women should be fully covered.

As Wahhabism took over as the state religion in Saudi Arabia, rules on clothing were gradually tightened. It is now one of the only Muslim-majority countries (Iran being the other one) to impose legally a public dress-code on women. All women in Saudi Arabia, locals and foreigners, must wear an *abaya*.

Mona Shehabi, a Jordanian fashion designer who has lived in Saudi Arabia since 1980, said: "The restrictions in terms of what women could wear in public started in 1990, at the time of the first Gulf War in Iraq. There was also growing pressure from the Wahhabi preachers. An increasing number of incidents of domestic violence resulted from women refusing to cover their face, particularly in Riyadh. In spite of this, many women continued to resist. Up until 1992 there were some women who did not even wear an *abaya*."

And so Saudi women have turned to another way to express themselves: they personalise these obligatory garments. Accessories are one channel for this, creating a demand that is being increasingly met by major fashion brands. Some women are even launching their own brands: last April, the Saudi government teamed up with Vogue for a showcase of the nation's most promising designers in Jeddah.

"In most cases these restrictions boost creativity," said Christophe Beaufays, a 33-year-old Belgian who has worked for five years in Jeddah as a fashion designer. "Jeddah is the most open city and

experimentation is in the air: many of the young, high-class women no longer wear a *hijab,* [to cover their head] in some public spaces, like restaurants or 'destination' malls. Their *abayas* are decorated, even partly coloured, and are made from cotton rather than heavy fabric. Some women have even been seen wearing white *abayas*, which make an extremely bold statement in this context." In Saudi society, white is traditionally only worn by men.

Technology introduces Saudi women to a wide range of brands and fashion blogs, and also gives them degree of protection. "The advent of technology has even made the religious police more cautious," wrote Susie Khalil, a US blogger who has been married to a Saudi for 40 years. "In a shopping mall in Riyadh [in 2012], local police detained and assaulted a Saudi woman who was wearing nail enamel while shopping. The woman refused to be intimidated, and she stood firm and reported the assault." After a video of the incident went viral online, the head of the Saudi religious police condemned the policemen's behaviour.

If women in Jeddah are gaining greater scope for self-expression, exactly

Some women have even been seen wearing white abayas, which make an extremely bold statement

the opposite is happening in war-torn Yemen, where the influence of Saudi-sponsored Wahhabism is spreading.

"Paradoxically, Yemen has always been more open than Saudi Arabia, particularly in Aden. The *abaya* doesn't form part of Yemeni tradition and it was only imported after the 1990s," added Marie-Christine Heinze, a German anthropologist at the Centre for →

OPPOSITE:
Women on the streets of Sana'a, Yemen's capital

ABOVE: Women waiting at a beauty salon in Yemen

→ Applied Research in Partnership with the Orient in Bonn, said: "The importation of the black *abaya* and *niqab* only occurred quite recently because of a burgeoning middle class that had identified the Saudi economic model for business with its regulations for outer dress.

"As soon as Saudi Arabia became the country where everyone dreamed of going

The abaya doesn't form part of Yemeni tradition and it was only imported after the 1990s

to make their fortune, middle-class women started to wear the black *abaya*, as a symbol of superior social status."

Rooj Alwazir, an activist and founder of #SupportYemen based in the capital Sana'a, has seen this trend first hand. She said: "I'm surprised both that women from the Old Medina find it strange and even offensive that a young woman should decide to wear traditional Yemeni garments, and also that my niece, who's now

15 and often goes to school without covering herself at all, is dying to wear an *abaya* in a coffee shop. But I can understand her: the in-fashion here in Sana'a is Saudi, even if all the fabrics are imported, many from Kuwait or Jordan."

For activist Bushra al-Fusail, wearing, or not wearing, an *abaya* was a question of survival and resistance. In May 2015 al-Fusail launched a Facebook event called Let's ride a bike. The idea was to encourage Yemeni girls and women to break a taboo and cycle. Fuel shortages, because of the war, had made driving all but impossible. They wore *abayas* so they were not seen to flout two taboos at once. "The campaign provoked a flurry of reaction, above all on social media," she said. "The least conservative told us we could use bikes, but only if we were well covered by *abayas*. However, as a matter of fact, the women who took part in the campaign do not normally wear them in everyday life. We need to break this reliance on certain in-built traditions, some of which aren't even ours." ⊗

Laura Silvia Battaglia is a freelance journalist living between Italy and Sana'a in Yemen

Rebel with a totally fashionable cause

45(04): 27/28 I DOI: 10.1177/0306422016685973

Model and journalist **Wana Udobang** refuses to conform to Nigerian dress codes, but finds this can lead to conflict

BENEATH MY BLACK wrap dress, my body had been bound and harnessed in a corset. My insides were choking, my ribs bruised and, unable to let out a breath, I unfastened the hooks of the corset and yanked it out from underneath me. That was the year of the Body Magic and thanks to Kim Kardashian we were all told that the hourglass figure was in. And every girl walked around looking like their chest was about to explode from trapped air.

That day my brother, his wife and I attended a family friend's wedding. We had refused to buy the *Aso-ebi*, a uniform dress that you wear during festivities and ceremonies to show some kind of solidarity with either bride or groom.

At the door, the bouncers didn't let us in because we weren't wearing the "uniform". We found a familiar face that beckoned to the bouncers to let us through. When it was time to be served, the food kept passing over our heads. Even the Chinese family wearing the *Aso-ebi* got served and we didn't. Then my sister-in-law found out the caterer was her stepmother, so at least our plates were furnished with a few crumbly leftovers. Finally, when the souvenirs were being distributed, we didn't get any. This is the kind of thing that happens to you when you choose to be a rebel.

ABOVE: Wana Udobang

Nigerian weddings are in many ways a microcosm of how our fashion choices intersect with access to society and our sense of freedom.

Growing up, everyone followed the same clothing trends usually dictated by music videos and US television shows. Whether →

the brand names which adorn your body have always been a key indicator of how much access you will be permitted into social circles, business cabals and pretty much everything else.

I left Nigeria as a teenager, attending sixth form in Dagenham, in the UK, where I first discovered chavs, punks, goths, and emo kids. I went on to study at an art college in Farnham where being different was what everyone strived for. For most of us, the stranger the better.

So you can only imagine the culture shock I experienced moving back home ten years later and often being criticised by my friends when embarking on a night out. I would usually get an eye scan from top to toe and then get asked: "Are you going out like that? This is not London. Oh please go and change and don't embarrass me." Unfortunately, since I live for embarrassing moments, my friends have gotten used to the fact that I usually wouldn't dress to the nines just to go have a few drinks down the road.

Though fashion might just seem as basic as wearing a bunch of clothes and expressing yourself, I often think that our very restricted clothing choices are also symptomatic of our restrictions in personal freedom. It is reflected in our near absence of niche markets in business and even the fear that people have in expressing any alternative points of view on subjects like religion and sexuality. I remember a story about a girl who grew up belonging to the Grail Message religious sect but often lied to people when asked whether she was Christian for fear of judgment or being ostracised.

In many ways, what has happened is that we have grown from playground groups to adult gangs. I often wonder if we are still seeking validation as well as acceptance and our fashion choices are only indicative of that. ⊗

Wana Udobang is a multimedia journalist, writer, poet, filmmaker and model

→ it was wearing your hair in Janet Jackson box braids or the Toni Braxton pixie cut or the boys in their lumberjack shirts and Timberland boots - if you weren't on trend you could never hang out with the cool kids. Since we barely had subcultures that grew out of rebellious clothing choices or alternative music movements, many had little option but to strive to be cool. And if

If you didn't make the cut you were deemed razz, which essentially is a synonym for lowbrow

you didn't make the cut you were deemed razz, which essentially is a synonym for lowbrow.

I find that our clothing choices share a link with our classist culture. You will often hear us use the term "dress the part" or "packaging", though it isn't restricted to fashion because it also encompasses your accent, the car you drive, the people you roll with. But the choices of clothing and

ABOVE: Two fashion models taking a selfie in Lagos, Nigeria

İSTANBUL İSTANBUL

BURHAN SÖNMEZ

ISTANBUL IS A CITY OF A MILLION CELLS, AND EVERY CELL IS AN ISTANBUL UNTO ITSELF.

Below the ancient streets of Istanbul, four prisoners – Demirtay the student, the doctor, Kamo the barber and Uncle Küheylan – sit, awaiting their turn at the hands of their wardens. When they are not subject to unimaginable violence, the condemned tell one another stories about the city, shaded with love and humor, to pass the time.

Set after a military coup, this powerful novel – translated into twenty languages – is an ode to Istanbul, celebrating the art of storytelling and the power of the imagination in the face of adversity.

'A writer of passion, memory and heart, Sönmez revives not only the stories of a land but also its bruised conscience.' ELIF SHAFAK

**30% off when you buy online at Al Saqi Bookshop
Visit www.alsaqibookshop.com to claim offer***

Discount code: Istanbul2017

*Valid until 31 March 2017

£8.99 ◆ Fiction ◆ Paperback ◆ eBook available

TELEGRAM
www.telegrambooks.com

26 Westbourne Grove, London W2 5RH
T: (020) 7221 9347: F: (020) 7229 7492

45(04): 30/31 I DOI: 10.1177/0306422016685975

Rowson

MARTIN ROWSON is a cartoonist for The Guardian and the author of various books, including Coalition Book (2014), a collection of cartoons about the UK's years under a coalition government

Ethiopia in crisis, closes down news

45(04): 32/35 | DOI: 10.1177/0306422016685977

As Ethiopia declares a state of emergency, **Ismail Einashe** explains some of the history to the current situation

For Oromos, Irreechaa is their most significant cultural event, and even though they are evenly split between Christians and Muslims, they all share ties to the original Oromo faith, Waaqefanna.

But at this year's festival there was a stampede and attack by the Ethiopian police. The numbers killed are disputed – the government said 52 were killed, but activists from the Oromo Federalist Congress claim 678 people died.

And since pictures of the festival goers who were killed were published internationally, the state has shut down all access to the outside world.

Behind the tragedy at Irreechaa is a long history of the Ethiopian state repressing Oromos, said Dr Awol Kassim Allo, an Ethiopian lecturer at the UK's Keele University.

"What is going on now in Oromia is a massacre in the name of emergency,

OPPOSITE: Demonstrators chant slogans during the Irreechaa festival of the Oromo people in Bishoftu during October 2016, before the police started firing on festival goers

What is going on now in Oromia is a massacre in the name of emergency, terrorising civilian populations

ETHIOPIA HAS BEEN in lockdown for months. There has been a state of emergency declared and there is little news coming in and out of the country. Social media and the internet have been outlawed, religious and cultural events banned, curfews imposed. Thousands of soldiers are roaming the streets.

It escalated after security services started killing people at the annual Irreechaa festival for the Oromos in Bishoftu in October 2016

This thanksgiving celebration of the Oromos is attended by millions from across Ethiopia and the diaspora. They wear traditional clothes and sing songs of resistance.

terrorising civilian populations to force them into capitulation," he said.

He added: "The massacre at Irreechaa occurred before the state of emergency, although Ethiopia has always been under a state of emergency, the official declaration of emergency was a conclusive evidence that the state was losing control and that a large segment of the society has rejected the government's authority to govern".

Celebrating their traditions and wearing traditional dress, as the Oromos were doing at Irreechaa, has historically been part of the resistance to the government in Ethiopia, according to Mohammed Ademo, founder and editor of OPride.com, a multimedia →

OPPOSITE:
Oromo women at
October's Irreechaa
festival where oppo-
sition activists say
678 people were
killed by security
forces

→ news site focused on Ethiopia's Oromo community, and now based in the USA.

Recently, many Oromos have begun to eschew Western attire completely and wear Oromo clothes. Oromo clothing has been more visible on the streets. This way of dressing is becoming a cornerstone of their identity and self- expression.

Traditional Oromo clothes consist of *woya* for men, which are toga-like robes, usually white, and a skirt called a *wandabo* for women. Oromo women also wear *qollo* and *sadetta*, cotton cloths traditionally hand-spun and hand-woven, and sometimes other garments are worn such as leather or animal skin robes.

On Facebook there are numerous groups now dedicated to dissecting the latest fashion styles of Oromo dress and there are popular style blogs that enjoy a huge following. Latest pop hits by Oromo artists heavily feature Oromo clothes – along with dances.

Peri Klemm, a professor in African history of art at the University of California at San Diego and expert on Oromo dress, said: "At times when identity is threatened, dress, particularly that of Oromo women who have always been the carriers of culture, becomes a way in which the Oromo maintain a sense of who they are."

He and his friends had to share secret codes to evade state censors. They wore red, green, yellow beads

The Oromos are one of Africa's largest ethnic groups and constitute about a third of Ethiopia's 100 million population. But, despite their numbers, they have complained about political, economic and cultural marginalisation within Ethiopia.

For the last couple of years Ethiopia has been rocked by huge anti-government protests led by the Oromos against Ethiopia's authoritarian government.

The unrest was sparked by the Addis Ababa Integrated Master Plan, a plan to transform Ethiopia's capital city. Addis Ababa is surrounded by Oromia state, one of the nine ethnically based regional states in Ethiopia. Oromos said the plans would displace farmers, and this would be an attack on Oromo identity.

Prime Minister Hailemariam Desalegn has admitted that as many as 500 anti-government protesters may have died in police crackdowns and stampedes since protests began, but the opposition say the true figure is much higher.

During his student days in Addis Ababa in the 2000s, Ademo recalls that whenever he wore his traditional Oromo clothes, people in the streets would stare at him with suspicious eyes. In Ethiopia, he told Index, "there is this mindset that to wear Oromo cultural clothes is a threat to the state".

Ademo remembers that wearing Oromo clothes could be too overt. He and his friends

used beads and bracelets to share secret codes to evade state censors. They wore red-green-yellow beads to mark the colours of the Oromo Liberation Front flag, a political movement founded by Oromo nationalists in 1973. Ademo said to avoid detection by the state people wore these beads, necklaces and bracelets showing the red of the Oromo flag – which also has a sycamore tree, star and yellow stripes in the middle.

He added: "If a person is wearing a bead on their neck or a bracelet, you know they are likely Oromo." For women who wear the traditional skirts, to show the colours on their skirts could mean arrest. "If the colours at the bottom of their skirts are the colours of the resistance, you will get arrested," he said.

"When people have no other ways of expressing themselves, they turn to showing their resistance through clothes, without necessarily saying they are resisting," he said. Klemm said these kind of symbols are particularly powerful now: "In today's struggle for land and equal governance, the image of the sycamore tree has become a vital symbol of pan-Oromo identity, during the Oromo *gadaa* system of governance, representatives of the Oromo nation gathered under *odaa* trees".

He added: "Due to the current curfew, restrictions of movement, the outlawing of all social media, and the banning of mass gatherings of Oromo for religious, political, social, or cultural reasons, Oromo protest songs have [also] become a significant vehicle to reach and empower people."

For Ademo watching the attack on the Irreechaa festival unfold was an "attack on Oromo identity". Many in the diaspora have called this a massacre, and for them Irreechaa has now come to represent "a very traumatic moment in Oromo history". ⊗

Ismail Einashe is a freelance journalist based in London. He tweets @IsmailEinashe

Baggy trousers are revolting

45(04): 36/38 I DOI: 10.1177/0306422016685978

Fashion historian **Katy Werlin** examines how new styles of clothes played a significant role in the French Revolution

"**WE ARE THE** *sans-culottes*... poor and virtuous, we have formed a society of artisans and peasants... we know who our friends are: those who freed us from the clergy and from the nobility, from feudalism, from tithes, from royalty and from all the plagues that follow in its wake..."

On 8 September 1793 the *sans-culottes* society of Beaucaire, a militant group that rose to prominence during the most violent years of the French revolution, gave this rallying cry. But it wasn't through words and actions alone that they stamped their mark on history. What they wore also made a powerful statement.

The name *sans-culottes* translates to "without breeches", referring to the more casual trousers worn by the working classes. The *sans-culottes* expressed their new freedoms through their clothing, transforming dress which had been a mark of poverty into a badge of honour. They proclaimed to the world that their clothing, once a sign of oppression, was now a sign of freedom.The people had found a voice and suddenly the ordinary, the "artisans and peasants", became extraordinary.

What the *sans-culottes* claimed to have stood for and the reality of their actions are two different things. But they do provide a fascinating look at a group who used clothing to celebrate the freedoms brought about by the French revolution, a conflict lasting from approximately 1789 to 1799. It is difficult to describe the social make-up of the *sans-culottes*, a radical and often violent faction whose most active years were between 1792 and 1794. Ostensibly the faction was filled with members of the labouring and lower middle classes - small shopkeepers, artisans, craftsmen, and those who did heavy manual labour, though their ranks were later swelled by sympathetic small landowners. They idealised a simple existence where all citizens were equal. But the defining feature of the *sans-culottes* was not the participating social classes or ideology, but their dress.

As it had been in the centuries before the French revolution, dress was a potent visual indicator of social status in the late eighteenth century.

Fabric was extremely expensive, and an elegance of appearance was associated with an elegance of character. Being well dressed was a significant investment, both financially and socially. Fashionable dress for men was a three-piece suit consisting of a coat, waistcoat, and breeches. A man's status was shown through both the fineness of fabric and trims as well as the tailoring.

CREDIT: Archives Charmet / Bridgeman Images

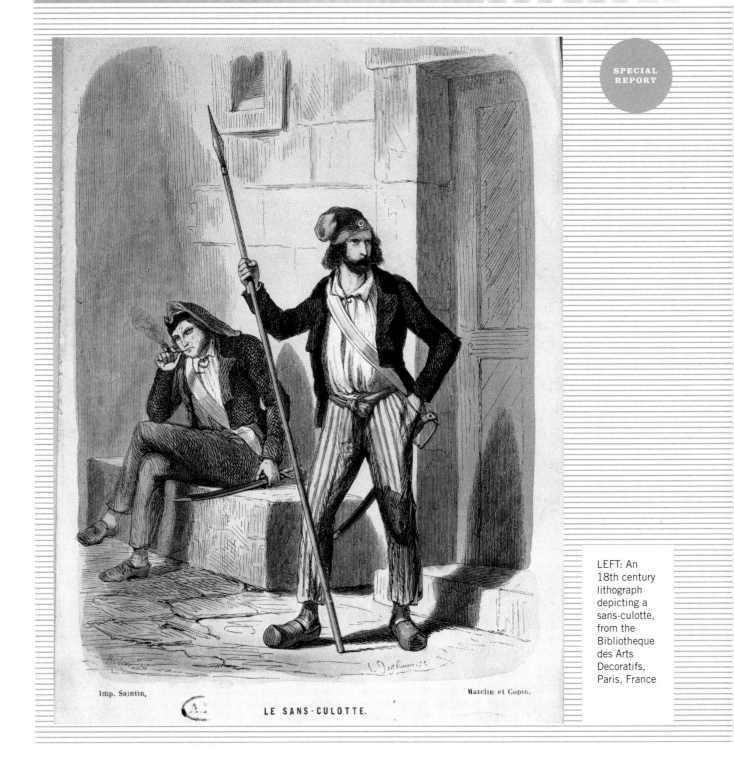

LE SANS-CULOTTE.

Imp. Saintin,

Mazelin et Copin.

This was before the age of fast fashion. Everything was handmade to order. A suit would be sewn to the exact measurements of the customer, ensuring a perfect fit. The ability to afford such tailoring was a show of wealth as well as lifestyle. Well-fitting clothing was restrictive, thus a man in a perfectly tailored suit was a man of leisure.

The dress of the working class was different to that of the nobility and bourgeoisie – clothing was looser, allowing for the movement required of manual labour. The basic components of coat and waistcoat remained, but the tight breeches were replaced by loose fitting trousers (*le pantalon*) to allow for more freedom of movement. It is from this significant difference that the *sans-culottes* took their name. In addition, the typical uniform of the *sans-culottes* included a short jacket (*le carmagnole*), wooden shoes, (*les sabots*), and a red cap of liberty (*le bonnet rouge*).

The dress of the *sans-culottes* was →

→ not new or different, it was the same style of dress which had been worn by the working-class for years, but the context had changed. As author and fashion historian Kimberly Chrisman-Campbell said: "Their working-class trousers served as shorthand for their radical pride in their humble origins and egalitarian values. In many ways, it was comparable to young people proudly wearing torn, distressed, or

Dressing in the sans-culottes style became a way to express visually loyalty to the revolution

sagging pants today: a deliberate and highly visible rejection of authority and polite society in general."

Ironically, the anti-fashion statement of the *sans-culottes* became a fashion in itself. Some members of the bourgeoisie and the elite adopted the *sans-culottes* uniform as a way of showing sympathy with the revolutionary cause. Philippe Halbert, a Yale University history of art doctoral student, said: "There was something 'fashionable' about the *sans-culottes* even as they eschewed aristocratic sartorial conventions." Dressing in the *sans-culottes*

style became a way to express visually loyalty to the revolution, an increasingly important statement during the violence of the reign of terror, when loyalties were constantly questioned and even wearing the wrong colour could lead to imprisonment or execution.

The celebration and revering of lower-class dress by the *sans-culottes* reflected the celebration of egalitarian principles by the revolutionaries. Before the French revolution members of the lower class had no voice. They had minimal representation in government and there was a huge economic disparity between the nobility and the common people. The press was highly censored and there were very few avenues for an ordinary man to speak out against the system. The French revolution, despite its violence, also gave the common people a voice. New representative government systems were formed, allowing more citizens an active role in deciding their fate. The press flourished and hundreds of newspapers were published. The celebration of lower-class dress by the *sans-culottes* was a celebration of these new freedoms of expression, socially, politically, and economically, that the revolution promised. Despite their noble ideology, the reality of the *sans-culottes* was very different. Their cries for freedom and equality only truly applied to white men, and women were discouraged from the *sans-culottes* movement.

The *sans-culottes*' activity leading up to and during the 'reign of terror' gave them a reputation also as one of the most militant and bloodthirsty factions of the entire revolutionary conflict. Yet despite the level of violence and chaos in the revolution, many great changes came about and the *sans-culottes* represent an important moment in the history of political fashion and its relationship to revolution. ⊗

Katy Werlin is a fashion and textile historian. She writes about fashion history on her blog

RIGHT: A painting of a stone model of the Bastille carried by four sans-culottes on Bastille Day, 1792

CREDIT: akg-images/Fototeca Gilardi

Muslim punks in mohawks attacked

45(04): 39/43 I DOI: 10.1177/0306422016685979

In Indonesia, punks face everything from savage beatings to compulsory head shaving and "re-education". **Eliza Vitri Handayani** looks at their struggles to retain their style

PUNKS IN INDONESIA negotiate many identities. Some Muslim punks wear mohawks over their hijabs. Others shave theirs off before entering mosques or coming home to see their parents. Others do not care at all and sport their punk attire and bare their tattoos everywhere they go.

Often, they are discriminated against based on their appearance and there is an increasing backlash against punks from conservative forces in the country. In June 2016, the Demak branch of Nadhlatul Ulama, Indonesia's largest Islamic organisation, banned reggae and punk concerts because they make young people "dress weird" and "stay out all night".

And in the most famous crackdown on the punk scene, which sparked actions of solidarity from punk communities across Indonesia and around the world, Acehnese police arrested 64 punks, shaved their heads, and forced them to pray and bathe in rivers to purify and re-educate themselves.

There are many reasons young people in Indonesia are attracted to hardcore/punk: the loud music that lets you scream your frustration, the do-it-yourself idealism that encourages learning by doing, the defiant attitude that gives the middle finger to a world filled with greed and discrimination.

Some are involved in social or political issues. Jerinx, drummer from the punk band Superman is Dead, has been actively protesting against the large-scale reclamation and development of the Benoa Bay in Bali, a project also widely resisted by local communities for its likely destructive effect on traditional fishing.

The band Marjinal has held concerts for victims of forced evictions in Jakarta by governor Basuki Tjahaja Purnama. Kolektif Betina, a gathering of women in the

Hera's mother stopped talking to her for months when she found out Hera had tattoed her arms

hardcore/punk communities, mounted LadyFast, a festival and safe space to discuss sexism and ways to overcome it.

Many punks in Bandung, West Java, start clothing lines or *distros* which are places from where magazines, indie music labels and DIY crafts are distributed. Fashion designer Risma Adhelia, set up her own clothing line, Rismakill Drama Darkcloth, offering stylish gothic outfits for →

→ everyday wear. Risma makes dresses, harnesses, corsets, garter belts, cage bras, and other "sick-ass kinky playthings". Risma used to be into punk, now she's more into black metal. She started making such items for herself, as she couldn't find them in Indonesia. She also made gothic wedding dresses for rent and modelled them for photographers.

"At first nobody wanted to work with me, they told me the pictures wouldn't sell and models were supposed to be thin, tall, and fair-skinned, not covered in tattoos," she said, "But now I get calls from many photographers and clients."

While people such as Risma find more connections with kindred spirits via social media, conservative elements within Indonesian society are more vocal and visible than ever, and society in general is increasingly polarised.

Women, compared to men, face increased stigmatisation in society based on their looks. Risma often finds people assuming she can't do anything valuable, just from the way she dresses. Abused by her grandfather, Risma left home while still in high school and made a living by sewing and doing odd jobs. When her family found that she had done well, they suspected prostitution. "I considered it: I was a girl alone on the streets," she said. "But I felt I had other talents. I promised myself that I would show my family, I was not the shame they think I am." When she stayed in Makassar, South Sulawesi, her neighbours were utterly surprised that she could sew. "They didn't think someone covered in tattoos could have any feminine skills," she said. To prove herself Risma taught her neighbours to sew.

Every day she wears microskirts and fishnet stockings. She doesn't feel her style limits her movement or makes her unsafe. She talks back when people harass her. She admits, however, that she deliberately cultivates a mean persona, especially in the punk and metal scenes. "That way I don't get harassed, because guys think I'm scary and not sexy."

An initiative which makes fashion accessories started by Kolektif Betina was the punk collective Needle 'n' Bitch based in Yogyakarta, a city in Java central to the island's artistic and intellectual heritage. The group hold workshops on sewing, zine-making, and self-defence. Each

Police arrested 64 punks, shaved their heads, and forced them to pray and bathe in rivers to purify themselves

week members gather in their base-camp to sew or knit and bitch about everyday problems, from abusive husbands to mandatory virginity testing for girls and women. Needle 'n' Bitch makes tote bags, aprons, purses, and other accessories from leftover fabrics, imprinted with bold messages such as Love Sex Hate Sexism, Fuck Your Beauty Standards, and My Body My Choice. The merchandise is sold via social media and proceeds go to fund the collective's activities. By teaching their members sewing and brand management skills, Needle 'n' Bitch has become a source of empowerment for women, many of whom have limited other opportunities. At the same time it raises members' awareness of gender equality and women's rights.

Punk musician, blogger and film maker Hera Mary has been documenting the punk scene since she was 18. She shot a documentary on women in the hardcore/punk community in Indonesia called Ini Scene Kami Juga (We are Part of the Scene Too). The film showed that women still have to fight for the space to perform and be acknowledged as equals to men in the scene, not as mere fans or sex objects. The film was to be →

OPPOSITE: Mikhail Israfail, known to his fans as Mike, is the lead singer of the punk band Marjinal which has held concerts for victims of forced evictions in Jakarta.

→ launched at the LadyFast festival, in April 2016, but hardline groups wrecked the festival before a screening could take place. The protesters shouted that the women were prostitutes, satanists and communists. The police stood by watching.

Since then the film has been screened in many places across Indonesia. Hera said the men in attendance felt directly criticised, but many were willing to admit that the problems depicted in the film were real.

Hera said she hasn't experienced violence because of her style. She's had some heartbreak, though. Many punk men still see women in the scene as "naughty girls" and would only date punk women casually, later choosing a "goody-goody" woman for their serious girlfriend or wife. A boyfriend took Hera home to meet his parents, only to find his mother repulsed and incensed by Hera's

Needle 'n' Bitch members gather to sew or knit and bitch about everyday problems, from abusive husbands to mandatory virginity testing for girls and women

tattoos. Hera's own mother stopped talking to her for months when she found out that Hera had tattooed her arms. Hera is now married to another punk, whose family are devout Muslims, but they have never objected to Hera's tattoos, never even persuaded her to pray. All they ask is that Hera cares for their son.

Another empowering initiative in Bandung is the street library, founded in 2012 by a group of students and punk scenesters who wanted to share the books they had read with other people. Every Saturday night they unroll a mat in Cipakayang Park and lay their books for everyone to read. The well-lit park is a popular hang-out spot for motorcycle clubs,

WHERE FASHION ICON CHALLENGES POWER

ISMAIL EINASHE explains how the flat cap, once only worn by the Mafia in Sicily, is becoming a symbol of protest against organised crime

"I make him an offer he don' refuse. Don' worry," goes the famous line of Robert De Niro's character, Vito Corleone, in the 1974 film The Godfather II. The cult Godfather films portray the life and crimes of a mafia family in the USA, and the violence and extortion that goes with being in the "family business". In the second film, a young Vito Corleone appears wearing a *coppola* or cap, in a scene shot in Sicily. Long before the film came out, the Cosa Nostra, the Sicilian Mafia, had adopted the flat cap, previously the headwear choice of 18th century English aristocracy, as their own.

The *coppola* first arrived in Sicily as a gentleman's driving cap, but when, later, the Mafiosi began to wear it, the

skateboarders, punks, skinheads, metalheads, and other people. Visitors can stop and read at the street library's corner, or simply chat with each other.

In August 2016, about 50 military men arrived with guns and batons, and dispersed the crowd at Cikapayang Park and beat three street library activists. One of them was singled-out for wearing a nose ring. News of the attack brought public attention to the street library, gaining them thousands of new supporters and boxes of books in donations. People of Bandung placed a huge wreath of flowers at the library's spot at Cikapayang Park. "Almost 80% of those who expressed their support were literary people," said

CREDIT: Paramount/Rex

hat quickly became a symbol of The Family, taking on the criminal associations the group inspired. It came to be known as *la coppola storta*. Meaning bent or twisted, *storta* referred to the way in which the cap was worn. Wearing the cap at different angles marked your affiliation to a particular mafia group.

But in recent years there has been a movement to change the murky associations of wearing the *coppola*, and in Sicily the hat has gone from a mafia symbol to one of change and resistance. Fashion designer Tindara Angello who owns La Coppola Storta, a store in Sicily's capital Palermo, has led a charge to rid the island of the stigma of wearing the *coppola*. She told Index: "I want to change the *coppola* from a symbol of the Mafia to the renaissance of Sicily". This, she said, will not only revive the image of the *coppola*, but will help to change perceptions of the island itself, which has long been plagued by its Mafia associations. "I want the new style of the *coppola* to give a new image of Sicily," she added.

LEFT: Vito Corleone, played by Robert De Niro, wears a coppola in The Godfather II.

Eheng one of the street library activists. "I wonder if we weren't a library, would people be as supportive? The way I see it, no one deserves to be treated violently, not if you're a punk or whatever, even criminals must be treated lawfully."

Eheng said: "We choose to look this way, I don't feel I have to explain to anyone that we're good people. If you really want to get to know us, let's be friends."

While progressive movements are largely limited to the educated middle-classes, extremism often finds fertile ground among the disenfranchised, for example, the victims of mass evictions in Jakarta. Many previously voted for the current governor, but since

he's made 16,000 urban poor people homeless, he has seen up to 200,000 people rallying against him, accusing him of insulting the Koran. Underground communities such as hardcore/punk contribute to discussions beyond the middle class via zines, clothing lines, music, murals and visual arts, street libraries, and discussions at various basecamps and *distros*. By ignoring or cracking down on underground communities we are losing an opportunity to speak to a large portion of the nation. ⊗

Eliza Vitri Handayani is an author and translator. Her novel From Now On Everything Will Be Different appeared in 2015

Design is the limit

45(04): 44/46 | DOI: 10.1177/0306422016685980

China's government used to restrict what its people were allowed to wear. Now trends are outrageous, but fashion is not completely removed from politics, writes **Jemimah Steinfeld**

REACHING **HUISHAN ZHANG** is not easy. The fashion designer is racing between appointments as part of Paris Fashion Week. Before he has a moment to himself, he is taken off on a plane to his next set of appointments. Even his assistant is struggling to keep pace with his schedule. Such is the life of a Chinese fashion designer today.

Zhang is part of a new wave of fashion designers to emerge from China in recent years and as Zhang's schedule attests, they're in hot demand. They've become a staple on the global fashion circuit and their designs are worn by the fashion world's elite. Zhang counts actors Gwyneth Paltrow and Keira Knightley amongst his fans. Guo Pei, another famous Chinese designer, has dressed singer Rihanna; Masha Ma is loved by models Naomi Campbell, Georgia May Jagger and singer Lady Gaga.

Typically trained in the West, their favourite educational institutions being Parsons School of Design in New York and London's Central Saint Martins, these designers have

ABOVE: A young woman wears a plastic seedling accessory in Chengdu, China

been able to benefit from a more liberal and open China. Their styles are as much personal as they are cosmopolitan, differing from one designer to the next, and at times very daring. Of the designers Index on Censorship spoke to, none said there was anything they wouldn't be able to design. Providing they don't stitch political slogans onto garments, their clothes are canvasses where censorship does not exist and where the imagination can run free.

In a country where freedoms are hard won and where recent crackdowns on freedom of expression have reached artist communities, this is not something to brush off.

It has had a knock-on effect within Chinese society too. Take a stroll down Nanluoguxiang and this quickly becomes evident. Once a quaint alley in central Beijing, which 100 years ago would have seen women walking around with bound feet, the cobbled streets of Nanluoguxiang now heave with cool cafes and boutiques which cater to the city's avant-garde population. Style is serious business here. People wear anything from grungy, skater clothes to branded high street fashion, creating a cauldron of different looks. Playfulness is a firm feature. Two years ago young women could be seen wearing cat ears. A year later it was plastic plants. Comparisons with Harajuku, the shopping district of Tokyo known for its outlandish style, are easy to make.

"The Chinese market is willing to discover new styles. Chinese customers are not conservative at all, especially the younger generations. They're very open-minded," said Liushu Lei, one half of the label Shushu/Tong.

"The party has retreated from the details of people's lives and people are now enjoying plenty of personal freedom, including what to wear. Anything I wouldn't wear? I wouldn't wear a suit because that's just not me!" says Lijia Zhang, author of Socialism is Great! Zhang came of age in the 1980s and has watched China change.

"Even in early 80s, fashion was very politicised. Labaku – bell-bottom trousers – were labelled as 'bourgeois trash'. I never had a promotion during my 10 years at the factory because my bosses thought I wore a perm. In those days only people with bourgeois tendencies would wear a perm," says Zhang.

As Zhang highlights, the transformation of Chinese fashion is recent. Most date the

Providing they don't stitch political slogans onto garments, their clothes are canvasses where censorship does not exist

changes back to 1996, when the fashion designer Ma Ke established her ready-to-wear label Exception de Mixmind, the first of its kind in China.

Before then, fashion was drab, form often giving way to function. It was also highly political. The 1920s and 1930s, when Shanghai became known as the Paris of the East, were a brief interlude in a century otherwise dominated by conformity. The peak of this domination happened under Chairman Mao. At the heart of his vision was a country where everyone was equal in mind and appearance. Out went the *qipao*, the traditional figure-hugging Chinese dress, and in came the ubiquitous Mao suit. Personal adornment, be it jewellery or make-up, was banned and any transgression not tolerated.

When Mao died in 1976 and Deng Xiaoping took over, the party repositioned itself. Market reforms called for a new approach to commerce and with that fashion. Initially this was more geared towards the export market. Then, as the economy took off, so too did domestic fashion.

To be sure, fashion alone cannot compensate for the lack of political freedom in China. But on a personal level it has →

ABOVE: Men wear Mao suits at a train station in China in 1982, a period when strict rules restricted fashion, and Western styles were severely frowned upon

→ played a crucial role in fostering self-expression, individuality and confidence for the Chinese population at large. Designers know this and have used their new-found fame to expand on this. Singer and designer Gia Wang, for example, has a T-shirt line that features images and phrases about sexual empowerment. Masha Ma is known for making proclamations online, such as when she posted to her Weibo account: "Be yourself, you don't have to fake anything."

And yet for all its freedoms, fashion is not entirely removed from politics. The movements of the party continue to reverberate throughout society right through to the runway. In recent years, fashion has been particularly shaken by Xi Jinping's anti-corruption campaign. The campaign was launched when he came to power in 2012 and sought to crack down on all forms of conspicuous consumption. Spending big on designer labels had been a staple of China's rich and powerful. It is now passé and Western brands have seen sales figures slide as Chinese designers' sales have risen.

The anti-corruption campaign also coincided with a government call to move away from "made in China", bywords for cheap, mass-produced products, to "designed in China". People are being encouraged to support home-grown brands, and designers encouraged to act as ambassadors for China. "There's great championing of the idea that China can use soft power, their creative expression, to move forward out of the manufacturing rut," said Tim Lindgren, a designer who works between Australia and China. "The opportunity for local designers is ripe right now."

Lindgren draws attention to an uglier side of Chinese fashion. Like other industries in China, *guanxi* or good connections are important. All legal documents, from work contracts through to lease of land for workshops or stores, must go through government officials. Even Chinese fashion weeks are run in partnership with the government.

"If you wish to build a business with any bricks and mortar, you need to be on at least speaking terms with officials," he explained, adding that Ma Ke's husband is politically correct and because of that she gets to dress Xi Jinping's wife.

Lindgren goes on to tell Index about a designer who was on the wrong side politically. Helen Lee, now a successful designer whose label is stocked by the luxury Hong Kong and Chinese fashion retailer, Lane Crawford, encountered several hurdles when she was starting out. First, her warehouse was taken away from her to become a coffee shop as part of Shanghai's redevelopment in 2010. Then, she had to pay a hefty sum to participate in a fashion week the same year, with the first two rows of the show being allocated to officials. There was no space for her clients as a result. These same rules apply today.

"If you keep your eye on the money, who is paying what and why, it's not quite working the same way as here," Lindgren said. ⊗

Jemimah Steinfeld is a contributing editor to Index on Censorship and will shortly be joining the magazine as deputy editor

A modest proposal

45(04): 47/49 | DOI: 10.1177/0306422016685982

As "modest fashion" becomes increasingly popular in Turkey, representations of veiled women in magazines are provoking a major public debate, finds **Kaya Genç**

IN ISTANBUL'S INTERNATIONAL airports, metro stations and public squares, similar advertisements welcome you to the city: a blonde, north European-looking woman wearing a stylish veil gazes dreamily at the viewer. The same image is also a regular item in a new wave of fashion magazines. But beneath the glossy images a public debate is growing about the role these publications play in Turkey's social life.

In a country where the dividing cultural and political lines between secularists and conservatives seem increasingly dramatic, the growth in the visibility of garments for conservative women has turned into a key talking point both in Turkey and abroad. "Modest fashion" refers to garments considered to be in line with Islam's principles and understanding of modesty. The term applies also to fashion targeting Orthodox Jewish, conservative Protestant and Mormon women; some even consider Kate, Duchess of Cambridge as a modest fashion icon. But this broad definition is debated vigorously in Turkey, and in conservative circles, the question of who draws the line between "modesty" and sexiness has become increasingly more pronounced.

Berin Tuncel is a psychologist who writes columns for Aysha, currently the leading name in the field of "modest" fashion magazines. She told Index on Censorship: "As Muslims, we are experiencing an era where

the spiritual is being deconstructed." Tuncel said. "This is a test for us." For Tuncel it is crucial that conservative women express themselves via their garments, but this freedom of self-expression carries with it responsibilities.

Aysha straddles both conservative Muslim society and liberal Western culture. In May, the Istanbul Modest Fashion Week took place at Haydarpasa, a railway station from Ottoman times. Featuring products by more than 75 fashion designers and a line-up of top models in the modest fashion industry, the event was attended by Spanish beauty queen Natalia Ferrer Fernández and prominently backed by the magazine. The September 2014 issue of Aysha featured a cover interview with Emine Erdoğan, the wife of Turkey's conservative President Recep Tayyip Erdoğan, and contained a portrait of Tanju Babacan, the gay fashion designer who has recently begun working for Turkey's first lady.

While the week was a success, other such events have excited considerable controversy. Modest fashion magazine Ala (the name means "beautiful" in Ottoman Turkish) had already been severely criticised for its glossy, somewhat suggestive images of veil-wearing women when its editors announced the Ala Fashion Party in 2014. Here, things came to a boiling point. The party was scheduled to take place at Istanbul's →

→ Sheraton Hotel with the participation of DJs and a famous Turkish star. Ticket prices were reaching £1,000.

Islam, a religion of moderation, did not allow such excesses, a columnist from the Yeni Şafak newspaper argued, and then the party was abruptly cancelled. When three months later the magazine came up with a cover featuring a Swedish model, the criticisms were even harsher. "This is one of the

Atatürk asked his people to wear Oxford shoes, remove their fezzes and put on fedoras. Women were asked to dress like European ladies

magazines that 'sells happiness in exchange for money' to the secular women of the world," a columnist complained. "It is about time some said 'stop' to this lack of etiquette. Tomorrow can be too late."

The rise in modest fashion has both political and economical reasons. According to a Global Islamic Economy report, in 2020 the spending on modest clothing will grow to $327 billion, so the market is ever growing, and the entrepreneurially minded conservatives support this type of Islamic consumerism.

Clothes have been an intensely political subject in Turkey since at least 1829, when Sultan Mahmud II came up with a law concerning how statesmen should dress in the Ottoman Empire. The Sultan ordered his subjects to replace turbans with fezzes, and gave specific instructions on the colour of veils women were allowed to wear.

Almost exactly a century afterwards, Mustafa Kemal Atatürk, the founder of the modern Turkish state, enacted the first of his dress codes in 1925. Atatürk famously gave a sermon in Anatolia where he asked his people to wear Oxford shoes, remove their fezzes and put on fedoras. Women were

asked to dress like European ladies.

Such "modernising" measures continued throughout the 20th century. Following the military coup in 1980, for example, the new governing junta ordered that, with regards to "the clothing and appearances of personnel working at public institutions... female civil servants' head must be uncovered".

"As a result of this history, conservative women in Turkey were focused on being invisible instead of translating their identity into an image," Tuncel told Index. In her opinion, Turkish modernisation has been built on a process of de-veiling Turkish women and stigmatising conservative dress. "In television series and films, veiled women only played the roles of cleaning ladies or apartment attendants. This way a subconscious association was forged between veiled women and being lower class," she continued.

The tensions within the modern fashion movement have long fascinated Magdalena Craciun, an anthropologist from University College London. In her new book Islam, Faith and Fashion: The Islamic Fashion Industry in Turkey, Craciun explores the subject, building her arguments on the 15 months of fieldwork she conducted in Istanbul. There, she focused on what Islamic fashion means to different people: money, an opportunity for self-expression, or an ethical issue to be debated.

On several occasions, Craciun has attended fashion shoots for Islamic fashion magazines in Turkey. "I attended a fashion shoot. At this magazine, garments that did not reveal the flesh, except the face and hands, were considered modest." In addition, attention was paid to the make-up. "This is one way to materialise the boundaries of modesty... And one way to handle the issue of morality. From the editors' perspective, as long as they respected this boundary, then their work was within the limits of morality or the religiously acceptable."

However, even this working definition does not necessarily please everyone. "The final product, the fashion image, is a multi-authored creation," Craciun added. "It [involves] different agents; eastern European models, who knew nothing about Islamic modesty and employed their well-rehearsed repertoire of postures; the photographer, who had little or no experience of working with and for headscarf-wearing women..."

Modest fashion images have also taken over social media. "I would say there is a desire to dress fashionably, but also a concern over the public exposure through social media, Facebook, Instagram and Twitter," Craciun said.

"These young, fashionably dressed veiled women often express this concern. They might use different means to limit the public access to their personal posts.

She added: "There is a difference between the reaction that critics have to fashionable dress and the concern over over-exposure via social media."

Kübra Karakaş, a veiled fashion designer with more than a hundred thousand Instagram followers, feels the burden of the kinds of criticisms Craciun talks about. Karakaş, whose interest in fashion began in high school and turned into a career during university, told Index about "the unprecedented happiness that comes with realising one's dreams in life". But with this also comes a pressing sense of responsibility. "The pressure is sweet and perhaps even a good thing," Karakaş told Index. "Thanks to Allah, I have never received any rebuke from Islamic intellectual circles because of my Instagram posts. And there is a reason for that: my dresses are quite loose and I have my boundaries."

Karakaş's success is mostly due to the way she designs, wears and sells clothes using social media. She sees herself as part of this new entrepreneurial identity that combines stylishness and commerce in the field of modest fashion. "My visibility excites and scares me in equal measure," she said. "But for me this is not a bad thing at all. One has to think about her every step, and feel the

ABOVE: A model wearing a style by Malaysian designer Aidijuma during Istanbul Modest Fashion Week

excitement and fear together so as to avoid mistakes."

If modest fashion is a test for Muslim conservatives, as Tuncel said, not all have passed it successfully so far. But there is

If modest fashion is a test for Muslim conservatives, not all have passed it successfully so far

a growing sense among those who define their careers through these clothes that the responsibility falling on their shoulders is worth carrying so as to be able to find the right balance between how they look and how they feel. ⊗

Kaya Genç is a contributing editor to Index on Censorship magazine, and is based in Istanbul, Turkey

Uniformity rules

45(04): 50/53 I DOI: 10.1177/0306422016685983

New research from the USA suggests that what you wear affects how you think. **Jan Fox** looks at the psychological effects of prison uniform

PUNITIVE BLACK AND white stripes, echoing prison bars, were introduced to the US prison system in New York in the 1820s. Before the 1800s, most prisoners did not work and wore their own clothes. Today inmates sport every shade from denim blue to khaki to black and white stripes. Some prisons use the orange jumpsuit, reviled for its associations with the Guantanamo Bay detention camp, and now part of the context of hit TV show Orange Is the New Black.

But for many prisoners, clothing is degrading and humiliating, according to director of the American Civil Liberties Union national prison project, David Fathi. He said: "So much of incarceration is about stripping away your identity and I've been struck by how people in prison, where everything is terrible from food to medication to housing, cling to some shred of individuality and by how important clothing is to them.

"I know prisoners care about their clothing. When it's stained or dirty or ill-fitting (which it often is), it causes them distress and is just another gratuitous humiliation and form of depersonalisation that we inflict on prisoners while they struggle to retain some vestige of self-respect. Prisoners complain to me. It's notable. They hold up their clothing to me, full of holes and tears and tell me they've asked for a new one but can't get one."

Prison, in Fathi's view, should replicate the society to which prisoners are going to return. "More than 95% of these inmates will be getting out and living somewhere near you and we need to help prepare them, not demoralise them," said Fathi.

Long-serving Arizona sheriff Joe Arpaio, who lost his bid for a 7th term in office in November 2016, was well known for forcing male prisoners at his Maricopa County jail to wear bright pink underwear. When Tea Party supporters raffled off a pair of the same style pink underpants at an event attended by the sheriff, the proud winners declared they would have the pants framed and display them in their living room.

Needless to say Fathi is not a fan of Sheriff Arpaio's approach. "Personally," he said. "I see it as counter-productive to basic human dignity but we have very limited resources and can't fight everything.

"Since 1972 our mission has been to defend the rights of prisoners under the law to meet minimal standards of human decency and to roll back policies in the US that →

LEFT: A chain gang of prisoners in Arizona, USA

→ give us the highest incarceration rate in the world and we have to pick our battles.

"Incarceration in the US is a very decentralised process. We have 51 separate prison systems and thousands of jails so it's a Sisyphean task to deal with all complaints."

Monica Sklar, vice president of technology for the Costume Society of America, said: "It was the beginning of early industrialisation in the USA that led to the mass production of uniforms for prisoners, slaves and soldiers and was spurred on by the Civil War."

The practical purposes of prison uniform are well documented, but the psychological effects are less well defined. A UN declaration set down standard minimum rules for the treatment of prisoners in 1955, including the use of prison uniform. The rules were revised in 2015 under the newly named Nelson Mandela Rules which stated: "Every prisoner who is not allowed to wear his own clothing shall be provided with an outfit of clothing suitable for the climate and adequate to keep him in good health. Such clothing shall in no manner be degrading or humiliating."

One complaint that did get some attention and went beyond lack of freedom of

We feel a sense of difference when putting on any uniform, be it a lab coat, a police uniform or a prison jumpsuit

expression and firmly into the role of humiliation and control was a prisoner made to wear a see-through jumpsuit exposing his genitals and buttocks when being transferred from jail to the state prison system in Illinois. After his case was thrown out by the district court, the prisoner took his complaint to appeal, where it gained some traction. The court decided the jumpsuit might violate the prisoner's eighth amendment rights and could be considered "cruel and unusual punishment". Caught up in the red tape between the separate jail and prison systems however, the prisoner was unable to bring a case against the jail.

Abraham Rutchick is a leading light in the area of study known as "enclothed cognition"– roughly speaking the theory that clothes make the man. Rutchick, associate professor of psychology at California State University Northridge, explained: "We feel a sense of difference when putting on any uniform, be it a lab coat, a police uniform or a prison jumpsuit. Clearly there's a difference with prison uniform in that there's an interplay between issues like security and safety and obviously a reduction in personal freedom which includes freedom of expression. I'm a great proponent of the first amendment but it changes its meaning in this context."

In recent studies Rutchick and his team looked at the differences in perception of formal and casual clothes.

"The results showed a shift in those dressed in formal wear towards a more abstract focus which includes more long-term thinking and being able to delay taking small rewards for larger ones later on, whereas lower status, casual clothes showed a leaning towards more concrete ideas. In essence, the more powerful the clothing, the more abstract the thinking and the less powerful the clothing the more the wearer would not be thinking in broad terms but focusing on survival and day-to-day issues. It would be logical to conclude that in the case of prisoners who have a total lack of power, and vulnerability, this would be even more pronounced," he said.

Could this affect their chances of successful rehabilitation? While he knows of no actual evidence to support this idea, Rutchick, who is currently working on a new study into clothing which makes people feel less powerful, said: "It's reasonable to think an inmate is less likely to think about engaging in programmes that might be helpful in terms of rehabilitation, or something that benefits them later if we follow this line of thought about the importance of clothing."

Some inmates attempt to improvise with what they have in order to maintain a sense of individuality. Writing on the blog prisonwriters.com, Texas lifer Kevin Foster explained how fellow inmates, especially younger ones, use small details like different patterns in the lacing-up of trainers in a desperate attempt to express themselves.

"Defying the prison administration at every interval, you find shoelaces zigzagged, criss-crossing and hanging out wildly. Without Timberlands, guys shine up their black boots so tough that the sun reflects off of them. Some buy liquid wax to coat the boots with shiny gloss. The laces are blow out, dangling, maybe tied in braided loops, others with trinkets carved from pen tops or plastics to make it look like free-world medallions.

"Because what it means to be fully human is to have colour, flare and edge. Freedom of expression. What the inmate lacks in access to colours and sounds and smells, he makes up for with sharp creativity over the plain white, dull crew cut and wrinkled uniforms. Anyone who has walked within these walls (as visitor, resident or employee) will know exactly what I'm talking about," wrote Foster.

Improvisation versus depersonalisation is something that resonates with 23-year-old South Korean student Joo Young Kim, who recalls his compulsory national service on a lonely air base close to the North Korean border.

"We would do subtle things to our uniform like change the lace-up patterns in our boots, turn up our cuffs or collars – just to express our individuality," said Kim, currently studying English in Los Angeles.

Rutchick sees a common thread. He said: "I'm not surprised at prisoners or soldiers forced to do national service making modifications to uniform in any subtle way they can – we all want to express ourselves. If you make people unlike others [in society] they seek to be distinct."

Real life influences fiction. In the Emmy-winning TV comedy show Orange Is the New Black female inmates make shower

Defying the prison administration at every interval, you find shoelaces zigzagged, criss-crossing and hanging out wildly

shoes out of sanitary pads. The show has been such a hit since launching in 2013 that some prison authorities decided it had made the orange jumpsuit too cool, and have reverted to black and white stripes. They include Saginaw County jail, whose sheriff, William Federspiel told The Washington Post: "Lines get blurred between the culture outside the jail and within the jail. I have to do something to redefine these boundaries because they've been blurred far too often in public culture."

David Fathi would like to see prisoners allowed to wear their own clothes.

"North Dakota's prison system is now allowing this in certain circumstances. It's a small but significant step and I'm hopeful that we'll move further in this direction of continuing humanity," he said.

Meanwhile prisoners must make do with the uniforms they are issued. ⊗

Jan Fox is a contributing editor for Index on Censorship magazine. She is based in Los Angeles, USA

Keeping up appearances

45(04): 54/56 | DOI: 10.1177/0306422016685984

Novelist **Linda Grant** explains how her Jewish family always knew the value of dressing to impress

the authorities: tell them what they want to hear. Had they found themselves in the camp in Calais in 2016 they would be the ones caught out by the Daily Mail with a child refugee who didn't look, and wasn't, 15. Only after being settled in the country for 112 years do we feel comfortable telling the truth on forms.

None of my grandparents spoke the language (my grandfather who died in 1965 aged 92, would never learn much English and I communicated with him via my father's interpretation). They lived their whole lives huddled together in immigrant communities of like-minded co-religionists, shopped in kosher shops and built synagogues. They didn't trust outsiders and considered anti-Semitism to be a prejudice permanently endemic beneath the veneer of English politeness. In turn, they were considered to be pushy, prickly, demanding and insistently upwardly mobile.

My parents didn't have a very good opinion of the working class. Words have

OPPOSITE:
Thousands of Jewish people fled to the UK from eastern Europe in the early 20th century, among them Linda Grant's grandparents. This family settled in east London and are shown in a family portrait in 1915

My mother implicitly understood the symbolism of the designer label long before they became the objects of mass desire

I HAVE ALWAYS BEEN conscious of coming from an immigrant family. My grandparents on both sides came to Britain at the turn of the last century from the pogroms of eastern Europe. In the photographs taken just after they arrived, against the potted ferns and classical balustrades of a professional photographer's studio, they are beautifully turned out but indisputably foreign-looking. This display was put on with much the same purpose as their instinctive understanding of how immigrants should deal with

meanings beyond the dictionary. For them the *goyim* meant not just gentiles but people who were coarse, uneducated, drank more than a sip of alcohol, and ate terrible tasteless food without flavour. They were contemptuous of the workers who told you that they "knew their place" in the class system, who identified with the class they had been born into, were proud of its traditions and culture. My grandparents wanted nothing to do with being at the bottom, they were aiming upwards, as high as you like. Henry Higgins, in the film My Fair Lady, declares that →

→ you can classify an Englishman as soon he opens his mouth. My grand-parents knew that no amount of elocution would erase the guttural traces of Yiddish, but they had other means of differentiating themselves from the working class: their clothes. For a worker wore a cloth cap, a middle-class person wore a homburg hat. "There's only one thing worse than being skint and that's looking as if you're skint," was the motto they handed down through the generations.

Clothes were status as well as a sign of wealth. Their oldest son, my uncle, paid extra to have his initials blocked in gold letters in the inner sweatband of his hat. No-one could see it, but he knew it was there. It gave him an extra swagger. My

Unlike her larger, louder, sisters-in-law, she also learned how not to appear the caricature of the vulgar Jewess

father bought his suits at Austin Reed, made to measure. "The best of everything," he said. "Only the best is good enough for my family." On holiday he would march us up the steps of the five-star hotel we couldn't afford to stay in and herd us into the lounge for afternoon tea. Because we looked the part, we were taken to be the part. We were never turned back or greeted with suspicion. Maybe, yes, my father looked like a rich Jew, but that's what he wanted to look like.

My mother, who was a clothes horse from the very start, implicitly understood the symbolism of the designer label long before they became the objects of mass desire. She wore very little make-up, just some eyeshadow and lipstick, but in her ward-robe were the massed ranks of Jaeger and Aquascutum. How did she know what to

wear? She read the fashion magazines, of course. Unlike her larger, louder, sisters-in-law, she also learned how not to appear the caricature of the vulgar Jewess. My aunts went for it with a vengeance. They came to afternoon tea in silk dresses, mink stoles, ropes of pearls and diamonds and a parasol. If it looked like it was worth a few bob, they'd put it on. My mother achieved her greatest aspiration in 1959 when my father took her to an East End furrier who made her a Persian broadtail coat with white mink collar, velvet-lined pockets, a satin lining decorated with hand-embroidered rosebuds and her own initials. It was spectacularly stylish.

In later life, in reduced circumstances, my mother began buying clothes from charity shops. She had a very good eye and got some terrific bargains, but it seemed to be both a sad decline from former glory and perhaps a marker of her becoming a true Englishwoman: thrifty, charitable, no longer aiming for the skies. My parents understood how power and class were intricately linked in ways they could not intellectually explain. They knew because of the pragmatic reality of settling in an another country, freeing themselves from the shadow of oppression and murder. Like their reverence for education, they saw clothes as the means by which people like them could appear to be who they were not. Appearances were absolutely crucial, not shallow, superficial, valueless. Had they had the opportunity I don't doubt they would have worn brand new tweed jackets with brand new leather patches and taken to the grouse moors to ineffectually wave around a gun with absolutely no understanding of the contempt that would have accompanied them. It took another generation to get the layers of meaning that lie hidden in that greatest of English institutions, nuance and irony. ⊗

Linda Grant is a British author. Her latest novel The Dark Circle was published in November 2016

Sewing it up

45(04): 57/59 I DOI: 10.1177/0306422016685986

Fashion and freedom have both changed dramatically in the last six decades. Britain's oldest working supermodel Daphne Selfe talks to **Rachael Jolley** about what she has seen

DAPHNE SELFE WAS rediscovered as a model when she was 78. Now somewhat of a legend herself for helping to bust stereotypes about age, Selfe has worked with some of the biggest names in fashion from Jean Paul Gaultier to Katherine Hamnett.

As someone whose career stretches back decades, she has more knowledge than most about how changes in fashion have echoed changes in freedom of expression for women, and men, in British society.

Now 88, and still a regular in glossy magazines, Selfe has experienced many shifts in fashion both on and off the catwalk →

ABOVE: Britain's oldest supermodel Daphne Selfe

→ since she began her career in 1949. "In the 50s you had much more formal dressing – certain clothes for certain activities – you never went to London without hat and gloves and proper shoes and stockings. Tights were the big revelation. People began to bare more flesh."

She remembers that she had a bit more freedom and did wear trousers sometimes, "because I rode horses. I was always able to dress like that and that was acceptable". Women and girls did far less sport in her childhood and "men never wore shorts except for sport. What people wore on the beach, now is acceptable in the town".

A chat with Selfe is a bit like unlocking a series of scenes from British history from the 40s onward. There's a telltale chuckle and the stories roll out. As a child her mother would never, ever wear trousers, and she herself was only allowed to wear them "because I was in a dance group and we had them

She remembers in her early life women just never wore trousers except for the south of France set

for a number" as well as when she went horse riding. She remembers in her early life women just never wore trousers except for "the south of France set".

Women always wore hats, even to the cinema, she remembered, and if you didn't, well, "you were rather scorned – why isn't she wearing a hat, y'know? You had to dress accordingly or you were not let in to lots of places. You had to toe the line."

Toeing the line came in lots of different forms. She remembers a time when being gay was illegal, and although she worked with several gay men nothing was said publicly. "You would have kept it all secret. Gay men are not illegal any more, and that's a big step forward.

STYLE COUNSELS

Changes in fashion amplify shifts in society
LILY COLE tells KIERAN ETORIA-KING

"I think clothing allows us to express ourselves as individuals and assert and play with our sense of identity," said model and actor Lily Cole told Index.

"However, most people dress within the narrow conventions of their culture and so in many ways it is an artifice of freedom."

Ever since being approached by a Storm modelling agent while out for a burger in 2003, Lily Cole has quickly become an iconic face in fashion. She was model of the year in 2004 at 16, then headed for London Fashion Week and was the youngest model to appear on the cover of British Vogue.

"I actually don't know why but T-shirts are often the vehicle of political expression and statements: maybe because they are such casual items of clothing, cheap and gender neutral? Maybe because wearing a slogan on your chest is more impactful than on your legs or back! Whatever the reasons, T-shirts have almost created their own language and conversation."

She spoke of how for many people, particularly women, changes in dress codes have often been a reflection of significant periods of increased freedom and equality, or of repression. "The recent episode with the burkini in France is a poignant example of the politics of fashion," she said, referring to controversial by-laws which saw Muslim women on French beaches forbidden from wearing full body swimsuits. "The move from Victorian corseted dressing was paralleled by the evolving women's liberation movement in the West; getting the vote alongside 20s' flapper style."

Women will always seek to express their individuality. in conservative Muslim countries, despite severe restrictions on

Selfe, with her striking long grey hair, admits she could "look good in a bin bag" and then goes on to reveal on one of her shoots the designer actually crafted a ball gown for her out of three of them. She recently starred in the Channel 4 documentary Fabulous Fashionistas about women with an average age of 80 who love fashion. Her role in changing attitudes to older women, especially seeing women in their 70s and

LEFT: Lily Cole attending the BFI Luminous Fundraising Gala, at The Guildhall in London

You had to dress accordingly or you were not let in to lots of places. You had to toe the line

80s in shiny fashion magazines, is quickly glossed over. But she does acknowledge that yes, it is a big shift.

The model has seen fashion and clothing used in many different ways, something she talks about in her new book The Way We Wore – A Life in Clothes. She has worked with Hamnett, the designer famous for her T-shirts of protest: "Yes, I wore one of those." And more recently she was involved in campaign work with Oxfam and Jean Paul Gaultier to send bras and other clothing to Senegal.

What was the biggest change that she remembers? "Not wearing stockings and suspender belts but wearing tights. But not wearing corsets – wow!" Of course that unlocks a conversation about whether corsets are really restrictive and Selfe reveals that she is a fan of them, though they have to be fitted tightly or they are uncomfortable.

Times have changed and so have attitudes. "Now women are freer and do more exercise. So the clothing has definitely changed." ⊗

Daphne Selfe's new book The Way We Wore – A Life in Clothes is published by Pan Macmillan

Rachael Jolley is the editor of Index on Censorship magazine

their clothing, women show their fashion sense through shoes, handbags and jewellery. Cole has seen the same thing happen wherever people are restricted to a uniform.

"I was amazed once when standing at a degree ceremony watching all the girls go by in uniform, each with their own twist on style to create identity - some wearing heels, or jewellery, or make-up that distinguished them." ⊗

Tall stories

45(04): 60/63 | DOI: 10.1177/0306422016685987

In countries where there are tight restrictions on what women can wear, high heels can be one of the few ways to show a public fashion sense, argues **Sally Gimson**

AT THE MOST recent Dubai fashion week the organisers promoted chairs in the shape of high heels "for your bedroom", and the models for Saudi fashion designers walked the runway in stilettos. Heels are all the rage in the Middle East and popular with women who are struggling to find different ways of expressing themselves in fashion.

Meanwhile in Europe and North America, women are rebelling against high heels especially when they are being forced to wear them for work. They are even trying to get governments to change the law to stop employers making them compulsory.

So are high heels a way of expressing your freedom and femininity as a woman or are they a terrible constraint on women's movement imposed by men who want to control women and do not care if they suffer injury as a result?

Young female Saudi fashion designer Nora Aldamer, who won the Jeddah Vogue Fashion experience award this year for her Chador collection and was at Milan Fashion Week for the first time this autumn, sets her beautiful clothes off with heels.

Saudi Arabia is opening up to the wider fashion world and there is even some official encouragement to do so, but it is difficult. There are very strict religious rules about what Saudi women wear in public. They have by law to put on a full *abaya*, a black robe-like dress, when they go outdoors. Women are not allowed to drive cars and there is a strict guardianship system which prevents women doing vital tasks without the permission of a male relative.

Yet the one way women, even under their abayas, do express themselves freely is through their footwear. It is not uncommon to see the flash of a Christian Louboutin shoe from under the black robes of a rich Saudi woman.

Aldamer told Index that women have been taking care of their looks and following tradition but adding accessories from international fashion labels like heels since her grandmother's generation.

"I don't see it as a new trend," said Aldamer. "It's just that the spotlight has been on Saudi women lately following the political situation in the region. High heels are very important for Saudi women as a daily accessory as they have been for most societies until recent years when it has changed to more comfortable sneakers and flats. Still high heels are in every Saudi woman's closet regardless of social status."

Iran is another country where you can be stopped in the street for wearing the wrong thing. Women have to wear headscarves and have their arms and legs covered. There are, however, no restrictions on how high a woman's shoe can be.

Tala Raassi, an Iranian American

designer, was given 40 lashes in Iran at the age of 16 for being at a mixed party wearing a miniskirt. Now 35, she lives in Washington DC, has just published a book called Fashion is Freedom and designs bikinis. She said women in Iran wear make-up, accessories and high heels because they have few other ways of expressing themselves through what they wear. It is a way of following the religious rules without getting punished.

"High heels and make-up are the only way that women can express themselves. They can't show it through other fashion. Usually women wear lots of make-up, jewellery and high heels. It is showing their feminine side and they can feel sexy while following the rules and the laws," she told Index.

Fashion   restrictions   appear to be easing up for some young women in Tehran. The Instagram account for the Tehran Times shows photos of how some are pushing the boundaries of what is and isn't allowed, though as Raassi said this is still not the same as being able to freely choose what clothes you put on and what clothes you can take off.

Nevertheless, Rosie Findlay, a lecturer in cultural and historical studies at London College of Fashion, said that across the Muslim world there is a kind of negotiation for women between dressing modestly in accordance with their religion and dressing fashionably. Magazine Elle Oriental, for instance, is concentrated very much on beauty products and women's accessories such as high heeled shoes, make-up and handbags. "They are mixing things together. Muslim women are finding creative ways of expressing their identity through how →

BELOW:
Iranian women in Tehran watch a catwalk model

they dress, combining being modest and looking cool," said Findlay.

Helen Persson, the Swedish curator of the exhibition Shoes: Pleasure and Pain which is touring the USA and China, has said one of the most interesting things about heels is that for the last 100 years they have been an international phenomenon, worn by women regardless of culture to show their status, youth, wealth and modernity.

Yet while heels can be regarded in Saudi Arabia and Iran as a way of expressing individuality and freedom, in other parts of the world they are increasingly seen as a way of limiting women's freedom and even harming them.

It is some of the least well-off women in the lowest paid jobs who are being asked to wear heels, from receptionists in London to waitresses in fast food joints in Edmonton, Alberta in Canada.

Earlier this year a friend of one waitress at the Edmonton branch of Joey's restaurant posted a picture of the waitress's bleeding feet on Facebook, causing national outrage in Canada and forcing the company to clarify its policy. High heels were not obligatory, the company said. Wedges and flats were also acceptable and there had been a misun-

Heels can be regarded in Saudi Arabia and Iran as a way of expressing individuality

derstanding, it said.

Meanwhile, a receptionist in the UK was sent home without pay from a temporary job at city accountancy firm PricewaterhouseCoopers, which outsources its front of house positions through employment agency Portico (which has subsequently reviewed its policy) for refusing to wear high heels. She got her revenge by setting up a petition which has gathered more than 150,000

signatures calling on the British government to make it illegal for a company to require women to wear high heels at work. A committee of British parliamentarians took evidence about the matter and is due to report soon.

Nicola Thorp, the woman who set up the petition, said she was not taken at all seriously when she remonstrated with her supervisor, but had had a huge reaction to her story from friends and acquaintances who have had similar experiences.

Findlay explained why the imposition of high heels at work is problematic: "If you are not choosing to wear them yourself, it is more questionable. If high heels are part of the uniform, you might question why. It could not be about mobility and comfort, but it's probably about the sexual connotations of the shoe being a feminine article and being erotically appealing. That's why it is retrograde."

Women, she said, should be valued in the workplace for their capability, the way they do the job and other things which are much more important than looks. "We have moved away from the idea that the attractiveness of the women is a sign of a company's confidence and prestige, but it is still contested."

High heels were originally the preserve of the very rich in western Europe, and were a way for aristocratic women to show off their leisured status.

Persson said high heels for women and children became fashionable in the 17th century and by the mid-18th century aristocratic women sported heels as high as 12 cm. They were so elaborate and expensive that they were a way of flaunting wealth and the freedom that brought. But because women could not walk anywhere in the heels, it meant they were restricted in their own movements and totally dependent on others, servants and men.

As Persson told Index: "The heels didn't have a shank or a steel rod in them so you were tottering and had to go on the front of your foot so you didn't break the heel. Dancing was done on the point of your feet. It determined how you moved. You sat in your big dresses and looked pretty. You couldn't walk anywhere. You took two steps from the front of your house to your carriage."

It was only in the 1950s that high heels became available to all. Movement was much easier in them. Design had moved on so much that high heels no longer broke when you walked on them. They were, as Persson said, revolutionary and symbolised technological advancement. Advertisements showed women vacuuming and cleaning windows in high heels. They were sold to women as giving them freedom to do the house work while still being attractive to men. The US TV series Madmen highlights how this was also happening at work for women who were working in customer facing industries like advertising.

Consultant podiatrist Mike O'Neill from the College of Podiatry in the UK, said high heels were now recognised as causing damage not only to your feet but also your whole body: "For example, if you wear high heels day in day out and are on your feet like cabin crew and teachers often are, in the short term you are going to get blisters and sore feet, but in the long term you are shortening your calf muscles which can result in muscular problems and puts pressure on your joints and lower back. This can cause a range of mobility problems as you get older."

Interestingly the film industry is still one where heels are considered obligatory for stars. It is very difficult to get away with wearing flats on the red carpet and in Cannes women wearing flats have been refused entry to screenings. The film star Julia Roberts went barefoot on the red carpet at the Cannes film festival this spring to protest at their high-heels only policy.

And actress Kristen Stewart was quoted in Vanity Fair magazine, saying after she was made to take off her flats at the festival and

swap them for heels: "Things have to change immediately. It has become really obvious that if [a man and I] were walking the red carpet together and someone stopped me and said, 'Excuse me, young lady, you're not wearing heels. You cannot come in.' Then [I'm going to say], 'Neither is my friend. Does he have to wear heels?'"

As Stonewall, the British gay rights organisation, pointed out to members of par-

High heels are in every Saudi woman's closet, regardless of social status

liament, dress codes which demand high heels can also be highly discriminatory for people who identify as lesbian, bisexual or transsexual.

Yet high heels are still popular. Persson said high heels were the one piece of attire which is still symbolic of femininity and womanliness in the world and generally taboo for masculine men (though not of course for men wishing to express womanliness and femininity like Grayson Perry). There are notable exceptions like Lenny Kravitz who has divided the world of male fashion with his love of high heeled boots.

Findlay agreed that high heels and other shows of fashion may represent a sense of freedom for women and others who wanted to feel feminine, giving enormous pleasure, but they should not, she said, be imposed on women. "People are always telling women what they can and can't wear, what's appropriate and what's not. It happens in most cultures whether it is a religious mandate or an employer telling you to wear heels. This is part of a bigger problem." ⊗

Sally Gimson is an acting deputy editor at Index on Censorship

GLOBAL VIEW

45(04): 64/65 I DOI: 10.1177/0306422016685988

Jodie Ginsberg looks at how governments are curbing travel to stifle voices they don't want to be heard

RESTRICTING TRAVEL IS an old trick to curb free expression, yet it's a trick that persists despite the advent of the internet. Indeed, in some countries, such restrictions are on the rise.

Since the attempted coup in Turkey in mid-2016 and the introduction of a state of emergency, the country which is one of the world's leading jailers of journalists, has seized the passports not only of media critical of the government but also their loved ones. In September, Dilek Dündar, the wife of Turkish journalist and editor Can Dündar, was prevented by authorities from travelling out of Istanbul's Atatürk Airport. Her passport was confiscated and she was banned from going abroad where her husband had already fled. Her husband, former chief editor of the Turkish daily newspaper Cumhuriyet, had been arrested in

2015 on charges of disclosing state secrets, espionage, and aiding a terrorist group after he published videos and photos of arms deliveries by the Turkish intelligence services to Islamist groups in Syria. "The mob took my wife hostage," Dündar wrote for Index a week later.

Countries even stretch their arms beyond their own borders. Syria has used the passport system in an effort to punish those it considers enemies of the state, as was seen in the case of Zaina Erhaim, Index's 2016 Freedom of Expression Award Fellow for Journalism. Erhaim travelled to the UK for an Index-led panel event in September with veteran UK journalist Kate Adie. Erhaim's passport, the same one she used to join us for the Index awards five months previously, was confiscated on arrival by UK border officials because it had been reported as stolen by the Syrian authorities. When she asked how she might get her passport back, Erhaim was told to take the matter up with Damascus, a city she is no longer able to visit because she is blacklisted by the regime.

Though Erhaim was able to enter the UK, the passport seizure has made further travel highly problematic, which, as Erhaim told a press conference, is a very effective mechanism for stifling her. She has had to reject a number of invitations to speak at events throughout Europe in the coming

months where individuals who might not otherwise have encountered her journalism could have heard from her personally on the current situation in Syria.

The internet has enabled views and ideas to be shared more widely than ever before, but it has not yet successfully replaced the need for face-to-face contact as a means to share and debate ideas. That's why governments continue to use restriction of movement as a means to stifle freedom of speech, and why those who defend free speech must also fight every attempt by states to use travel bans or passport seizures to muzzle critics.

It is not just journalists or their families who find themselves subject to such restrictions. In April, Azerbaijani author Akram Aylisli, who was recently published in this magazine, was prevented from leaving the country to attend an Italian literary festival. Aylisli, who has incurred the regime's wrath for publishing stories about the massacres of Armenians in Azerbaijan, was detained at the airport and accused of assaulting border guards.

"Absurdly and illogically, this alleged incident of punching a border guard happened well after the plane departed and was later used by the border service as an explanation for denying the border-crossing before the plane had left!" he told Index. The speech Aylisli had been due to give was published on the Index website, but this is very different from hearing the man himself deliver his own words. At the time of writing, fellow Azerbaijani, investigative journalist Khadija Ismailova, is subject to a travel ban, as are other Index friends including former Freedom of Expression Award winner Nabeel Rajab of Bahrain and Malaysian cartoonist Zunar: all three prevented from travelling as punishment for their free expression.

While leaving a country can be difficult, entering it can be too. Italian playwright Dario Fo, who died in October 2016, was unable to travel to the USA for four years under the McCarran-Walter act, which restricted immigration. In September 1983, he was again refused permission to enter, and accused of "belonging to organisations supporting terrorist groups." As Fo later wrote in an article for Index: "The whole thing is absurd. My books are published over there and my plays performed, and the same applies to the other authors who are not allowed to visit the USA, but I'm banned from entering the country. It really is difficult to understand how someone like me can make America tremble merely by what I say. It is grotesque, a leftover from McCarthyism."

Lest we think such absurdities are now reserved only for Fo's playwright

Syria has used the passport system to punish those it considers enemies of the state

successors, in 2015 US rapper Tyler, the Creator was banned from entering the UK because some of the lyrics from old songs were considered as encouraging "violence and intolerance of homosexuality" and fostering "hatred with views that seek to provoke others to terrorist acts."

Countries that claim to uphold freedom of expression as a fundamental right must demonstrate that by also allowing freedom of travel, even for those whose views they find offensive, and whose views offend those of the dictatorships who seek to silence their critics by curbing their travel. ⊗

Jodie Ginsberg is the CEO of Index on Censorship. She tweets @jodieginsberg

CREDIT: Lucas Jackson/Reuters

IN FOCUS

IN THIS SECTION

MAIN: Press passes rest on a table inside of The Trump Museum near the Republican National Convention in Cleveland, Ohio, 19 July, 2016

Challenging media

45(04): 68/69 | DOI: 10.1177/0306422016685989

President Trump's record on the campaign trail raises the prospect of a full-scale attack on First Amendment rights and press freedoms, warns US media expert **Eric Alterman**

TO A DEGREE we've not seen before, the president-elect appears to have little respect for or understanding of America's tradition of freedom of the press, nor the protections offered the fourth estate under the First Amendment. Donald Trump has proven himself both an unashamed liar and a bully to those who reported unfavourably on his candidacy.

During his campaign, we saw tactics never used before by a political candidate. Journalists were confined to "pens" at political rallies and the crowd incited to throw insults at them. Trump egged them on, describing the media as "scum" and "among the most dishonest groups of people". He would shout from the platform: "We are living in a rigged system. And believe me, they are a big part of the rigging, those people."

Once in office, President Trump will have the power of the executive branch (at least) of the US government on his side. We fear what will happen next to freedom of the press in this country.

Many in the media hoped that Trump would "mature" after becoming president-elect, and discontinue the kind of attacks on the media that characterised his campaign. The first week after the election considerably dampened their optimism. He attacked the media in a tweet for allegedly "inciting" protests against him, as usual without evidence. He specifically attacked The New York Times on Twitter for reporting on problems with his transition. In another tweet, he alleged that the paper "is losing thousands of subscribers because of their very poor and highly inaccurate coverage" – a claim it flatly denies. The Twitter storm against the paper raged on for a while, before Trump finally sat down for an on-the-record meeting with its reporters and editors.

Trump's record on the campaign trail gives ample evidence that he and his advisers plan a full-scale attack on press freedoms once they enjoy the powers that come with his office. He has personally threatened reporters on the campaign trail, and promised to sue media companies over unfavourable coverage. At one point, he mused that the country needed to "open up our libel laws so when they write purposely negative and horrible and false articles, we can sue them and win lots of money".

Trump has issued threats to the owner of the Washington Post and barred its reporters from covering his rallies. A journalist from Vice was arrested for trying to cover one without permission. His former campaign manager Corey Lewandowski, later fired (and then hired by CNN), manhandled a female reporter for Breitbart News for the crime of trying to question him.

And then there are the threats – literally thousands of them – made by Trump supporters on the internet to reporters with Jewish-sounding last names who have sought to hold Trump, his family and his cronies accountable during the campaign. One such reporter, Julia Ioffe, who profiled Melania Trump for GQ, felt it necessary to contact the

local police as a result of the threats she received. Neither Trump nor anyone connected to him has done anything to discourage these threats. Melania Trump even accused Ioffe of "provoking" them with her reporting.

It's all but impossible to predict where President Trump's animosity to the press, coupled with the violent hatred he has provoked during his campaign, will lead. He often lies,

Journalists were confined to "pens" at political rallies and the crowd incited to throw insults at them. Trump egged them on

but he should probably be taken at his word when he says (as he did last June), "I am going to continue to attack the press."

Unfortunately, such attacks would occur at a moment when the US media are especially vulnerable. One reason is the rapid decline in the financial health of the newspaper industry, where most reliable news reporting originates. A related phenomenon is the explosion online, especially on Google and Facebook, of purposely propagandistic "fake news" sites that, as with Gresham's Law, drives out "good" or truthful news, frequently with nonsense supporting Trump's white nationalist agenda.

Coupled with the challenges the media face regarding public trust, barriers to truthful reporting and economic survival, the result of the 2016 election has left journalists less confident about the future freedom to report than at any time since the founding of the republic. Sadly, confronted with the unprecedented threats posed by a Trump presidency, confidence – perhaps more than any other quality – is what is needed. ⊗

Eric Alterman is a professor of English and journalism at Brooklyn College, and media columnist for The Nation

LEFT: A Donald Trump supporter wears a T-shirt with a threatening slogan at a campaign rally in Minnesota on November 6, 2016.

Living in limbo

45(04): 70/71 | DOI: 10.1177/0306422016685990

Award-winning filmmaker **Marco Salustro** describes the journalistic challenges of covering the plight of the thousands of migrants who have fled sub-Saharan Africa and are now being held in Libya

"**WHY, IF THEY** know they could die at sea, are they still coming?" That's the question being asked by many Europeans about the continuing flood of migrants trying to cross from Africa to Italy, Greece and other parts of Europe in crowded, often unseaworthy boats, many dying in the attempt.

I wanted to show what is happening on the other side of the Mediterranean, in Libya.

Working in Libya is difficult and dangerous, even with a good knowledge of the country and good connections. We didn't know what to expect.

What we discovered were hundreds of people being held in camps, waiting, hoping for a better life. Some were so thin that bones were sticking out of their backs. One woman told

us: "What will happen next, we don't know."

Migrants are keen to speak to the camera, desperately trying to call for help, to say: "We are here and we are human beings, we exist." In some way they believe that if only the world outside could know, something would happen to change things. They cannot believe they are just left to their fate.

These desperate refugees who have fled from terror in their own country (Sudan, Eritrea and Somalia) are housed in huge hangars. They are forced to live there, often with little water or food, and at risk of being beaten. Living in a halfway zone between home and the freedom they seek, they have no knowledge of whether they will ever leave Libya.

As part of the research for the story I

ABOVE: A group of migrants is detained under armed guard by militia men at an abandoned industrial park in Tripoli, Libya

needed access to government-manned centres, and authorisation from the ministry of interior. This often requires clearances signed by the police or other bodies, and includes days spent in waiting rooms and multiple telephone calls to different offices. Sometimes even that preparation was not enough, for instance on one occasion visiting the officially government-controlled Abu Slim centre, despite the visit being arranged by the ministry and an officer accompanying me, the militiamen, who weren't consulted beforehand, blocked our visit. As we crossed the gate a number of young guys wearing flip flops and carrying pistols threatened the director and the officers.

Of course, as there is no press freedom in Libya, we just scrape the surface and try to get as deep as possible, bearing in mind that what we can see is never the whole reality.

During my work, all the militias I met were keen to show how good they were at controlling the migrants and, astonishingly, they were not worried at all about hiding every kind of abuse they were perpetrating. In some way they seemed to believe that in Europe nobody cares about that, as long as they can prevent migrants arriving on our shores. In some cases the only reason I was allowed to work in one camp was because the militia thought that visibility of the media could have been useful to put pressure on the government.

The most scary thing is that what we were seeing and documenting was just the good part: what is shown is considered acceptable or even something to be proud of. Despite this, the living conditions I saw were really harsh and abuses are part of normal life. What happens out of sight may be even more terrible.

European public opinion was shaken when on 18 April 2015 more than 800 men, women and children drowned in the Mediterranean. Following this, the European Union expressed a willingness to bomb boats and ports used to smuggle migrants across

the sea. The Tripoli government, supported by Islamist coalition Libya Dawn, declared its intention to engage in the struggle against human trafficking, and started a campaign aiming to show it was serious about stemming the flow of migrants. The Libyan government is also receiving support from the EU to help control Mediterranean crossings.

Migrants have become a valuable commodity in the fight for power, as Libyan militias, who are widely believed to have a

Abuses were part of normal life. What happens out of sight may be even more terrible

major role in the human trafficking business, stepped into migration policy to try and gain influence on the government.

Government officials told me they did not have enough resources to carry out any of the operations the government had announced so they had hired rough militias "to secure the shores and stop illegal crossing to Europe."

The migrant stories are gruesome, they cannot speak freely and what we can hear from them is not the whole reality. The migrants I met with again when some of them managed to reach Europe told me about torture and killings as a day-to-day routine.

I thought it was important to cover this story to show what happens out of the sight of European people. While the public were demanding a bigger effort to save the lives of migrants in the Mediterranean sea, the actions undertaken by the Tripoli government to show itself as a reliable partner for the EU in the control of the migration flow were in effect worsening living conditions and increasing the danger for migrants in Libya. ⊗

Marco Salustro made the Vice News special Europe or Die, Libya's Migrant Trade and is the winner of the Rory Peck 2016 news feature award

Follow the money

45(04): 72/75 | DOI: 10.1177/0306422016685991

Imprisoned journalists make headlines, but the Turkish government has a more insidious method for controlling the media, argue researchers **Burak Bilgehan Özpek** and **Başak Yavcan**

ADVERTISING IS THE latest way for the Turkish government to lean on the media to stop critical stories going into the press, according to unpublished research.

The large advertising budgets of state-controlled Turkish industries like banks, telecoms companies and Turkish Airlines are being used by the government to develop a financial grip over newspapers and control what they report.

Patterns of advertising during 2015 suggest that newspapers which do not toe the government line, or are hostile, are being starved of those revenues.

For instance, Sabah, a newspaper particularly sympathetic to the government, received more than 20% of the advertising budget of the state-controlled bank Halk Bank, while the independent Hürriyet received only 2.9%, despite both having similiar circulation.

Government-controlled telecoms company Turkcell also favoured Sabah by giving it 9.4% of its advertising, while Hürriyet took just 3.1%.

The situation was similar for another state-controlled telecoms company, Turk Telekom: Sabah received more than twice Hürriyet's share of their total advertising.

New research found that any paper critical of the government – those associated with the social democratic movement, liberalism, Kemalism, nationalism, Islamism – was either discriminated against, or excluded entirely, when it came to crucial advertising revenue.

There was a clear inconsistency between the market share of the newspapers, as evidenced by their circulation, and their share of advertising coming directly from the state, or indirectly through state-controlled companies.

Research discovered that state-controlled companies' advertising policy was not in line with market forces: in other words, they did not choose to put advertising in newspapers according to those newspapers' circulation. Instead they chose the outlets according to how they reported on the government.

And this means that the newspapers' customers have become the state and

3.1%
9.4%

HÜRRIYET

SABAH

AD SPEND

Despite having similar circulations, state-owned Turkcell favoured pro-government Sabah with 9.4% of its advertising budget, while giving critical Hürriyet just 3.1%.

state-controlled companies, not their readers. As a consequence some newspapers have started reporting for the state's benefit and only publishing content of which the government approves.

Economic dependency of this kind has caused individual journalists and media organisations to give up their freedoms voluntarily. It has also imposed major financial penalties on those who want to continue exercising these freedoms.

The state and its companies have ensured positive coverage and increased public approval ratings.

The research was carried out by analysing the advertising spend of some of the leading state-controlled players including public banks such as Ziraat Bank, Vakıf Bank and Halk Bank; telecommunications companies such as Turk Telekom, TTNET and Turkcell; and Turkish Airlines. The companies are fully or partially owned by the state and their management boards are predominantly appointed by the government, although they act

State-controlled companies' advertising policy was not in line with market forces

as private entities aiming to maximise profits.

Although the exact amount of money spent by these companies is not transparent, information provided by the USA-based Nielsen Company, which monitors advertising worldwide, was used to approximate the total spend by measuring the number of ads (and their sizes in column inches) published in newspapers by Turkish state-controlled companies in 2015.

Using content analysis, the research then divided newspapers into three categories: pro-government, critical of government, and neutral.

The findings were very clear – and the researchers believe that this deeply entrenched asymmetrical economic dependence on the state by some Turkish media outlets is →

ABOVE: A man reads a newspaper outside a café in Istanbul

FREE SPEECH LOCKED UP

···

Linguist and newspaper columnist SEVAN NIŞANYAN has found himself locked up for 16 years after being subjected to a torrent of lawsuits relating to a mathematics village he was building. Researcher JOHN BUTLER managed to interview him

Well-known linguist Sevan Nişanyan will not be eligible for parole in Turkey until 2024. Locked up in the overcrowded Turkish prison system, he has found his initial relatively short jail sentence for blasphemy getting ever longer as he has been subjected to a torrent of lawsuits on minor building infringements related to a mathematics village he founded.

Nişanyan, who is 60, spoke exclusively to Index on Censorship. He said he was being kept in appalling conditions. Moved from prison to prison since being jailed in January 2014, he is now being held in Menemen Prison, a "massively overcrowded and brain-dead institution".

He added: "About two thirds of our inmates were recently moved elsewhere and the remainder pushed ever more tightly into overpopulated wards to make room for the thousands arrested in the aftermath of the coup attempt."

Nişanyan's ordeal started in 2012 when he wrote a blog post about free speech arguing for the right to criticise the Prophet Mohammed. Through notes passed out of his high security prison via his lawyer, Nişanyan told Index what he believes happened next:

"Mr Erdoğan, the then-prime minister, believes in micromanaging the country. He was evidently incensed.

"I received a call from his office inquiring whether I stood by my, erm, 'bold views' and letting me know that there was much commotion 'up here' about the essay. The director of religious affairs, the top Islamic official of the land, emerged from a meeting with Erdoğan to denounce me as a 'madman' and 'mentally deranged' for insulting 'our dearly beloved prophet'.

"A top dog of the governing party, who later became justice minister, went on air to assure us that throughout history, no 'filthy attempt to besmirch the name of our holy prophet' has ever been left unpunished. Groups of so-called 'concerned citizens' brought complaints of blasphemy against me in almost every one of our 81 provinces. Several indictments were made, and eventually I was convicted for a year and three months for 'injuring the religious sensibilities of the public'."

But what happened afterwards was even more sinister. He found himself, while in prison, facing eleven lawsuits relating to a village he was building with the mathematician and philanthropist Ali Nesin. Nişanyan has been

→ playing an important role in the decline of press freedom.

Few can argue that Turkish media was ever fully free, but balanced coverage and critical reporting have traditionally been considered important editorial norms by most journalists in the country.

But, as the ruling Justice and Development Party (AKP) has gradually consolidated its power, winning consecutive elections since 2002, press freedom has been in sharp decline.

Although those with an interest in free speech have been increasingly concerned by this, it was the reluctance of the mainstream media in 2013 to cover the extraordinary and unprecedented Gezi Park protests which made us, as media researchers, ask the question: "Why was the media so reluctant to report on what was happening?"

Of course one of the answers is coercion – but from this research we see the less overt, but equally effective way of limiting free

involved for many years in a project to reconstruct in traditional style the village of Şirince, near Ephesus, on Turkey's Western seaboard. It is now a heritage site and popular tourist destination. And nearby, he and Nesin have built a mathematics village which offers courses to mathematicians from all over Turkey and operates as a retreat for maths departments in other countries. They hope it will be the beginnings of a "free" university.

It was this project the Turkish authorities decided to focus on. Nişanyan was given two years for building a one-room cottage in his garden without the correct licence, then two additional years for the same cottage. Nine more convictions for infringements of the building code followed, taking his total term up to 16 years and 7 months.

He, and many others, are convinced that this is a political case, because jail time for building code infringements is almost unheard of in Turkey. He believes the authorities have prosecuted him for these crimes because they do not want his case to cause an international stir.

"Jailing a non-Muslim, an Armenian at that, for speaking rather mildly against Islamic sensibilities... would be a first in the history of the Republic," he told Index. "It might raise eyebrows both here and abroad."

Despite everything, Nişanyan is adamant that his time has not been wasted. He has been working on the third edition of his Etymological Dictionary of the Turkish Language, which presently stands at over 1500 pages.

On entering prison, he signed away most of his property, including the copyright to his books, to the Nesin Foundation which runs the mathematics village he is so passionate about. Today the village has added a school of theatre. A philosophy village is the next project in the works.

"The idea is, of course, to develop all this into a sort of free and independent university," he said. "I am sure the young people who have come together in Şirince for this quirky little utopia will have the energy and determination to go on in my absence."

speech has been the control of advertising. These mechanisms incentivise pro-government reporting and punish criticism.

Recent developments in Turkish politics, namely the failed coup in July 2016 and the state of emergency declared in its aftermath, have created an even more highly policed environment. By increasing the risks of critical reporting, these events have further accentuated the dependency structure.

As a result, there is little reason to expect the AKP government to relinquish its pressure on the media, unless major transparency and oversight mechanisms are set in place to regulate these kinds of state interventions. ⊗

A graph and further research from this project will be published on indexoncensorship.org.
Burak Bilgehan Özpek *is associate professor, and* **Başak Yavcan** *is assistant professor at TOBB University of Economics and Technology in Ankara*

Fighting for our festival freedoms

45(04): 76/78 I DOI: 10.1177/0306422016685993

Dealing with mutilated bodies, an attempted acid attack and speakers arresting each other. All part of his job organising Hay literature festivals around the world, explains **Peter Florence**

CREDIT: Daniel Mordzinski

RUNNING A LITERATURE festival in a context where freedom of speech is not a given is like playing chess on a plain grey board. Sometimes you are just not able to imagine where to move, and sometimes you just keep playing on grey. But as US President Barack Obama said so eloquently after November's election: "You say, OK, where are the places where I can push to keep it moving forward?"

Bringing people together around a table or a picnic rug or a campfire is a specific challenge. There is no mediated distance of print or broadcast. The whole point is that you're face to face, that you're making it personal. And the offence and the risk are as personal as the joy and the discovery. This makes it a fascinating challenge when the practicalities of running a big public event run into conflict with the authorities who license you to put up your stages.

Sometimes it comes like this: a week after a successful festival, a man you've been working with for a couple of years suggests a meeting in a café to review the year's work. He's a good man, an enabler; a man who has the careworn look of a bureaucrat who's survived in an undemocratic regime by knowing which battles to fight.

You like him, because he's helped navigate the public licences and public funding avenues. He orders cake. He enthuses about the opportunity to meet Hanif Kureishi at the screening of My Beautiful Launderette, and

VERACRUZ
GOBIERNO DEL ESTADO

veracruz
INCOMPARABLE

Universidad
Veracruzana

HAY FESTIVAL.ORG
ÁFRICA AMÉRICA ASIA EUROPA ORIENTE MEDIO

IN FOCUS

2-6 OCTUBRE 2013
HAY FESTIVAL

ABOVE: Hay Festival guests dancing in Mexico in 2013

the honour of hearing Carl Bernstein speak about the First Amendment. His funder is thrilled. They love the Hay Festival in the city. We're in a coffee shop, not his office. They are so thrilled they'd like to double the grant they give us. Alarm bells. Could we help them? Here it comes: could we programme the next festival just the same way, but without the homosexuals or the Jews?

Sometimes it's harder. Our first festival in volatile, thrilling Mexico comes to a world heritage site in Zacatecas, because the state's visionary governor has visited our festival in Cartagena, Colombia, and she wants to bring a similar experience to her home. The festival is a huge success. Her term ends and she is succeeded by a new governor who cancels all his predecessor's funded projects.

But across the country a dynamic new governor in Veracruz, Javier Duarte, picks up the baton and invites us to Xalapa. A fortnight before we start, a drug cartel dumps 35 mutilated bodies onto a busy road nearby. "It's a gang thing, an inter-narco incident," we're told.

We hold the festival. Tens of thousands of students come and listen and talk and wonder. →

ABOVE: Nigerian writer Wole Soyinka at the Hay Festival in Xalapa, Mexico, 2012

→ During the third year the talk about the Governor Duarte's probity starts. Journalists investigating the cartels are disappeared. We bring in Salman Rushdie, Jody Williams and Carl Bernstein again to speak up alongside Mexican writers. The students embrace the festival as a beacon of freedom of speech.

Year four, we receive a petition demanding that we cancel the festival and denounce the governor for failing to stem the constant steam of killings of journalists in Veracruz. The petition is signed by more than 300 journalists and some writers from across Latin America who have attended the festi-

Could we programme the next festival just the same way, but without the homosexuals or the Jews?

val. We listen. A rival, and much bigger petition is started by the students and teachers in Xalapa begging us not to leave, saying the festival is their bulwark against silence. But we cannot operate against the wishes of writers and journalists. We broadcast the festival digitally on BBC Mundo, and move to Mexico City and then to Querétaro. Many of the students from Xalapa come too.

Duarte is currently on the run from the police and the cartels.

Sometimes it's just farcical. In 2008, at our festival in Wales we invite George W Bush's confidant and former US Ambassador to the UN John Bolton to discuss Abu Ghraib and the "war on terror". Many supporters of Hay are appalled. Our good friend and neighbour George Monbiot, also a speaker, is so appalled he decides that he will attempt a citizen's arrest at the festival. I assume he's joking. Monbiot announces this is what he's going to do in The Guardian. The Dyfed-Powys Police inform me of the legal procedure for citizen's arrest and step away.

My mother reads me Voltaire. I brief our security team. The day comes. Bolton turns up. His interviewer is called to the BBC at lunchtime, so I have to go onstage with him. I ask him under what circumstances it would be OK for me, if I didn't believe his answers, to tip him backwards, bag him, and pour water over his face. He doesn't answer. He cannot say "under no circumstances", though I'm not sure he understands that's the issue. It's on YouTube; it's compelling.

Bolton knows that Monbiot is going to try to make a citizen's arrest, and George knows I cannot allow him to do that and still hold Hay as a platform for free speech. So that's what happens. We restrain a liberal hero from silencing an illiberal neo-con. A guy who throws a bottle of acid hits me, not Bolton. George writes a brilliant and widely shared account of why Bolton should be charged. At the time of writing, Bolton was said to be under consideration for the role of Secretary of State in President-elect Donald Trump's administration.

Hay Festival is 30 in 2018. We'll be celebrating by arguing for freedoms of speaking and reading. The festival continues to run around the world in Mexico, Colombia, Ireland and Spain. ⊗

Peter Florence is the director and co-founder of the Hay Festival

International Conference on Freedom of Conscience and Expression in the 21st Century

22-23 July 2017, Central London

Join notable free-thinkers for an historic International Conference on Freedom of Conscience and Expression in the 21st century on 22-23 July 2017 in Central London.

Speakers include Mukto-Muna's **Bonya Ahmed**, Filmmaker **Deeyah Khan**, Playwright **Gurpreet Kaur Bhatti**, FEMEN Leader **Inna Shevchenko**, Physicist **Lawrence M Krauss**, Algerian Sociologist **Marieme Helie Lucas**, Council of Ex-Muslims of Britain Spokesperson **Maryam Namazie**, Scientist **Richard Dawkins**, Author of Blasphémateur **Waleed Al Husseini**, Moroccan-born Charlie Hebdo Columnist **Zineb El Rhazoui** and many more.

For more information: www.secularconference.com.

Barring the Bard

45(04): 80/82 I DOI: 10.1177/0306422016685994

On the 450th anniversary of Shakespeare's birth, the Globe Theatre launched an ambitious production of Hamlet, attempting to perform in every country on earth. Actor **Jennifer Leong** recounts how they dealt with attempts to censor or edit performances

ABOVE: Leong (second from left) and the Hamlet company warm up for their final shows back at The Globe Theatre, London, after two years on the road, April 2016

IT WAS TEN o'clock on a hot December morning in the small, dusty village of Mandjou in eastern Cameroon. We had set up next to a street vendor's shelter, using his storeroom as our dressing room and the patch of ground outside as our stage. Kids who really were supposed to be in school had started to gather and that brought the grown-ups too. They were a French-speaking crowd of Cameroonians and many displaced people from the Central African Republic. A year and a half into a two-year world tour to take Hamlet to every country on earth, we were ready to steam on with a song and a "Who's there?"

Except we didn't get very far before the police tried to stop us. Inevitably, I suppose, it was in the middle of the iconic words almost synonymous with Shakespeare - Hamlet's "To be or not to be". The crowds were growing, spilling into the thoroughfare, and the police demanded to see our permit.

Having taken this play to 189 countries and reached people beyond that, we came to know every show day as a trouble-shooting day. When the issue was with location and crowd management it was, as with that singularly surreal day in Mandjou, expertly dealt with by our producer and stage managers. On other occasions we faced censorship panels that wanted to scrutinise anything from costumes to specific scenes or even the use of certain words and props. In trying to put on the same production everywhere, we experienced these cultural differences first hand.

Our project was the biggest tour ever attempted by any theatre in the world and it marked the 450th anniversary of Shakespeare's birth. Over two years our company of 16 travelled with all our set, playing everywhere from Azerbaijan to Zimbabwe. As with many touring productions we often submitted the script, complete with cuts and music cues, to the local theatres and relevant authorities for clearance and the preparation of surtitles. Sometimes the content or the presentation of our Hamlet came under scrutiny that was beyond that. In certain countries social and religious conventions demanded that we adjust aspects of the production simply for the show to go on.

One thing I discovered was that often we were being held to stricter standards than the average citizen. And no wonder, our show was often an "event" on the city's social calendar, a foreign company on a highly visible platform.

One of our stops was in Male, Maldives. White powdery beaches and waters of a deep shade of emerald? No. I couldn't testify to that, as we spent most of our brief stay there working, but we did have an interesting run-in at the airport. The state religion

of the Maldives is Islam, and there are rules against the display of religious symbols not belonging to the faith. As our set, housed in 16 bespoke trunks, passed through the airport scanners, an official looked concerned and asked the whole party to step aside. He had seen the golden cross that the priest holds during Ophelia's funeral towards the end of the play. We were not

We faced censorship panels that wanted to scrutinise anything from costumes to specific scenes or even the use of certain words and props

allowed to take the cross past customs and had to leave it at the airport, to be picked up on our flight out.

This was not entirely unexpected and we quickly made the decision to have the priest come on with just a black prayer book, which we had anyway for various other scenes when Hamlet was reading. The word "Christian" was subsequently cut from its few mentions in the play. In my opinion the changes did not affect the story we were telling; we got to put on a show for the Maldivians, complete with the rather subversive notions of appealing to a (Christian) God, and sublime philosophising →

BELOW: Leong performing at the Saitama Arts Theatre, Japan

→ about heaven and hell. The essence of the spiritual struggle was all there, despite the odd word being cut.

Performing in Tehran, Iran, was a more choreographed affair. It wasn't the first censorship panel we faced, but together with Pakistan and Saudi Arabia, it was one of the few occasions where we had to make changes to our costumes and blocking.

We were lucky to have words that, after 400 years, still start debates

We gathered at the theatre a couple hours before our normal call time to get into costume and greet the panel. While the men donned their usual Danish military garb, the women had to abandon our normal short-sleeved, fitted dresses completely. Headscarves were carefully pinned down, and we thanked our lucky stars that we decided, last-minute, to pick up some long-sleeved tunics at Lahore airport before jetting into Tehran.

Another aspect that came under scrutiny was physical contact between men and women onstage. The panel wished to see the nunnery scene and the closet scene, both depicting an intensely intimate encounter between two characters of the opposite sex. They also asked to see the dumbshow, our "play within the play" sequence in which Player King and Queen danced together, suggesting sexual desire and great intimacy. We toned down the dumbshow and made slight changes to the blocking of both nunnery and closet. I had noticed how the officials seemed more comfortable with Hamlet's violence towards Gertrude and Ophelia than the tenderness he felt for them leading up to the confrontations. The compromise in the end turned out to be, as put memorably by one of the panel, "You can touch but you cannot enjoy the touching".

One of the most rewarding things in negotiating all this was the response of our audiences everywhere. Many local writers and artists came up to us after shows, some visibly surprised, others simply excited, that they had just seen what they didn't think could be done on stage in their country. In Iran they saw men and women interacting as equals. In India they saw a young man and a young woman looking for love and trying to defy their elders. And in Saudi Arabia, Horatio, who could be played by either a man or a woman in a rotating cast in our production, was seen by the audience as a woman dressed as a man, getting involved in all the action.

I am rather proud of our record of never having to cancel a single performance over the two years. We did what was necessary to carry on doing the show, and never compromised on the story we were telling. It definitely helps that Shakespeare belongs to all and is beloved by all. We were lucky to have words that, after 400 years, still start debates, and still set pulses racing. ⊗

Jennifer Leong was a cast member of The Globe's world tour of Hamlet

BELOW: Leong chats to younger members of the audience after the show in Mandjou, Cameroon

CREDIT: Amanda Wilkin

Assessing Correa's free speech heritage

45(04): 83/86 I DOI: 10.1177/0306422016685995

As a decade under Ecuadorean president Rafael Correa comes to an end and elections approach, **Irene Caselli** looks at his record, from giving sanctuary to Julian Assange to his controversial media laws

TEN YEARS AFTER coming to power, Ecuador's President Rafael Correa is on his way out. The February 2017 election will mark the first vote in a decade without his name on the ballot. Since taking over in 2007, Correa has polarised opinion. While depicting himself as a guardian of free speech by granting Wikileaks founder Julian Assange asylum in the Ecuadorean embassy in London, the president has also made a point of silencing journalists at home. As he prepares to leave office, what is Correa's free speech legacy?

Correa has repeatedly said the media were his "greatest enemy". From the start, he used lengthy Saturday television broadcasts, modelled on the famous addresses by his ally former Venezuelan president Hugo Chávez, as his main platform. On the surface, the shows appeared to foster transparency and government accountability by detailing the administration's work and the president's ideas. But they soon turned into a source of controversy. Over the course of almost 500 speeches, Correa has literally torn private newspapers to pieces, attacked journalists by calling them "wild beasts" and referred to one female journalist as a "horrible little fatty". As well as the verbal abuse, he has

successfully sued media organisations, cartoonists and investigative journalists. "The president decided from the first moment that his fight was going to be against the media," argued Orlando Pérez, chief editor of the state-owned newspaper El Telégrafo. The newspaper, which belonged to a banker who went bankrupt, became Ecuador's first state-owned newspaper in 2008. As in much of Latin America, the private media in Ecuador represents strong economic interests and usually adopts a conservative stance. But Correa turned things upside down and has created a large network of state-run media. Pérez claimed that Correa's fight was necessary in order to guarantee the right to freedom of expression for each Ecuadorean citizen. "Citizens did not have any protection from the media," he said. Others disagree and believe this was not the motivation for the changes.

When new media laws were approved in 2013, the controversy deepened. Critics say the laws concentrated media in the hands of the government. They accuse the new media watchdogs, which are also under the government's control, of exercising censorship. The independent media freedom organisation, Fundamedios, →

ABOVE: Ecuador's President Rafael Correa sings during his weekly live broadcast in Manta, Ecuador

which is highly critical of Correa, has calculated that since the laws were enacted three years ago, 398 sanctions have been imposed on media outlets, of which only eight have been imposed on state-owned media organisations. "In 2013 we came under a regime of prior censorship," Cesar Ricaurte, Fundamedios' director, told Index. "The government discourse is based on the issue of plurality, but that remains only a discourse. We have more concentration and less plurality. Official propaganda almost entirely dominates the agenda. The private media are cornered and the community media are on the verge of extinction."

As a result of this restrictive climate, journalistic standards have gone down, said investigative journalist Christian Zurita. He co-authored the 2010 book El gran hermano (The Big Brother), which detailed government contracts benefiting the president's older brother, Fabricio. As a result, Zurita lost a US$10 million lawsuit

filed by the president, who later pardoned him and his colleague. Zurita told Index he used to work on 35 investigative features a year. Now that he works on an independent website, he is down to one a year. "There are things I can investigate, but I don't get paid for them," he said. A book like the one he co-authored in 2010 would be unthinkable in the current climate, he added.

"What's the role of a state if not to guarantee rights?", asked Paulina Mogrovejo of the National Council for the Regulation and Development of Information and Communication (Cordicom), one of two government-run watchdogs created by the media laws. "It would be wrong for the state to have weak public policies. Information is the most sensible common good." Mogrovejo said that the laws' four main objectives were to avoid concentration of media and to give more representation to minorities, improve quality, fight against discriminatory programmes and promote Ecuadorean

CREDIT: AP/Press Association / Martin Mejia

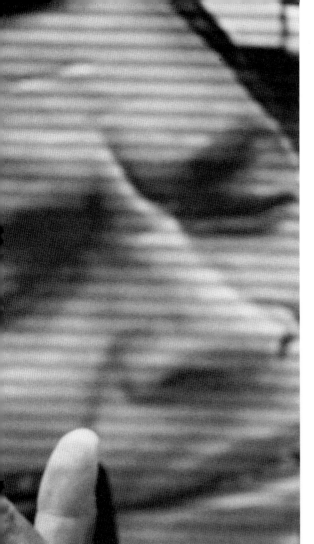

content. Among other things, the 2013 laws redistribute frequencies for radio and TV, giving 33% to private broadcasters, 33% to state media, and 34% to community radio stations run mainly by indigenous groups. But Fundamedios said that the assignation of frequencies, which is currently ongoing, is not truly pluralistic. "There is no transparency in the process, and there are no places for those critical of the government," Ricaurte claimed.

Criticism comes even from within Correa's own circle. "We're starting to feel a lack of plurality," said Samuele Mazzolini, an Italian-Ecuadorean academic at the University of Essex and former government consultant under Correa. "There is a growing unwillingness towards debate and dialogue." After he stopped working for the government, Mazzolini published a weekly column in El Telégrafo in which he often criticised Correa and his policies.

But in September 2016, he resigned

because of another El Telégrafo article which caused a stir: a piece by Anne-Dominique Correa, the president's daughter, who studies political science in France. The article, headlined The Art (or Science) of Disqualifying Democracies, criticised democracy rankings, questioning their Eurocentric worldview vis-a-vis Latin American governments. Pérez, the paper's editor, said it was Correa's daughter who sent him a copy of the piece, which was initially in French. "Correa would never call me directly," he told Index. "It would have been an act of censorship not to publish the piece just because it was written by the president's daughter."

The column caused a stir. "When the daughter of a president publishes her third-year university homework uncritically supporting her dad's theses in the pages of the state-owned newspaper amid magniloquent publicity, then I suspect that some sort of degeneration has taken place," Mazzolini wrote on Facebook. This led to disparaging attacks over social media, with the president himself stepping in and referring to Mazzolini as a "little clown".

The next column Mazzolini wrote for

Correa has attacked journalists by calling them "wild beasts" and referred to one female journalist as a "horrible little fatty"

El Telégrafo was not published. When he asked why, he was told his position was being assessed by the paper's editorial board. That is when he resigned. "Within the government party there is an asphyxiating atmosphere. Criticism is lived like an insult," Mazzolini explained.

The internet has also turned into a battlefield. Fundamedios has studied tweets →

→ by several government users, including Correa, highlighting more than a thousand insulting or menacing messages against the media. Spanish company Ares Rights, which was allegedly acting on behalf of the government, had several Twitter accounts and websites critical of the government suspended using US copyrights laws. Online magazines such as the independent news site, 4pelagatos, have reported online attacks.

The private media are cornered and the community media are on the verge of extinction

The government has also clamped down on whistleblowers, in apparent contradiction to the decision to grant asylum to the Wikileaks founder Julian Assange in 2012, who faced arrest in the UK and possible extradition to Sweden on charges of sexual assault. Correa has said he was offering support to the Australian anti-secrecy campaigner on humanitarian grounds, to defend him from the threat of political persecution. But things are not so simple.

"Correa took in Assange because of a genuine desire to back a progressive cause, and because he was on the same page as Assange in terms of his aversion towards the USA. However, there was no genuine desire to make the workings of the state more transparent," said Mazzolini.

"It was a huge propaganda operation and now it remains a hot potato the government doesn't know how to deal with," said Ricaurte. Hacking or leaking documents is illegal in Ecuador. Ricaurte mentions the case of Fernando Villavicencio, a journalist who wrote a series of investigative features alleging cases of corruption within the state-run Petroecuador oil company. Villavicencio also leaked documents, including some regarding

Assange's difficult stay at the embassy and plans to escape. Correa sued him and Villavicencio now faces charges of hacking and a possible prison sentence of up to five years for contempt of court.

As the elections come closer, everybody's eyes are now on Lenín Moreno, the governing party candidate who served as vice-president under Correa. Although the opposition is divided among many candidates, it is unclear whether Moreno has enough backing to win in the first round of voting, since polls show that Correa's credibility has gone down. A run-off vote could further complicate Moreno's chances.

Even within Correa's own camp, opinions vary as to how much the upcoming elections can change the current situation. Mogrovejo, of the national media watchdog Cordicom, believes that Correa's policies are here to stay. "The victories we have achieved through the media laws are backed by the entire Ecuadorean society, and they will be defended by the audiences which are every day more critical of the junk TV that private media impose," she argued.

Critics of Correa believe that even if the opposition were to win and the next president were to scrap the media laws, there would still be much more to do in order to create a healthy media scene in Ecuador. "We need a change of paradigm in order to recover good journalistic practice after years of silencing and self-censorship," said Zurita. He said his hope lies within the independent websites such as Plan V, 4pelagatos, Focus and MilHojas which have emerged over the past few years as the only platforms for criticism and reports investigating the government. "Despite bad news and difficulties, there are readers that want to find out about important issues," he said. ⊗

Irene Caselli is a freelance journalist living in Argentina and a contributing editor for Index on Censorship magazine

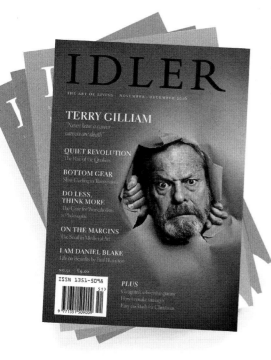

Framed as spies

||||||||||||||||||||||||||||||||||||||||||||||||||

45(04): 88/90 I DOI: 10.1177/0306422016685996

Steven Borowiec speaks to journalist **Choi Seung-ho**, director of a new documentary about South Korea's spy agency and the increasing difficulties for investigative reporters

CHOI SEUNG-HO HAS long been one of South Korea's most controversial journalists, but this year he raised his public profile to a new level. What has brought him to broader public attention is Spy Nation, his first feature-length documentary, an intense film about forced confessions of spying involving the National Intelligence Service, South Korea's main spy agency.

Of all the audience feedback he has heard in screenings around the country, Choi told Index, it is the shocked reactions of the middle and high school-aged viewers that are most memorable. "They are seeing their country's dark side for the first time, seeing things that the schools and media keep hidden," he said, looking fatigued but alert at a restaurant in Seoul, at the end a long day of screenings.

Spy Nation zooms in on the stories of men whose lives unravelled when they were accused by the NIS of gathering intelligence for North Korea. The men, many of them leftist activists and intellectuals, say they experienced physical and psychological torture at the hands of the NIS.

RIGHT:Journalist and filmmaker Choi Seung-ho at his office in Seoul

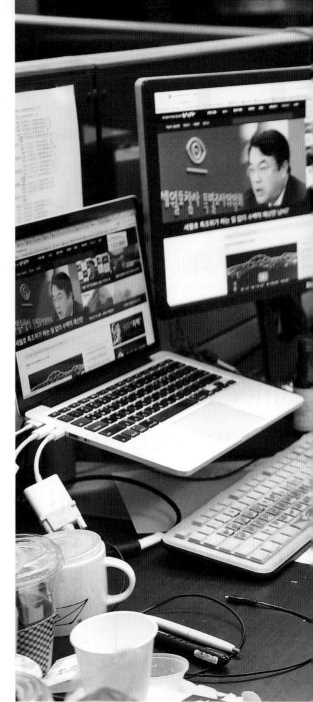

Though fighting in the Korean War ended in 1953, South and North Korea never signed a peace treaty and are technically still at war with each other. This means that both sides remain on alert, maintaining huge militaries. The NIS argues that its work is necessary to protect South Korea and prevent infiltration by North Korean spies.

On screen, Choi has a rough-edged style that is unusual among journalists in South Korea, where open confrontation with public officials is rare. Choi spends much of Spy Nation on camera, waiting outside the offices of NIS officials, then accosting

IN FOCUS

them seeking comment on alleged cases of people who say they have been framed for being spies.

The film became an unexpected success for an independently produced documentary, bringing in more than half a million dollars and drawing high-profile press coverage abroad. Choi explains that his story of spies has hit a nerve in his country, and drawn attention to a neglected problem. "We see this all the time in our society, this tendency for conservative governments to demonise their opponents by accusing them of being on North Korea's side," he said.

They are seeing their country's dark side for the first time, seeing things that the schools and media keep hidden

While encouraged by the strong response to the film, he remains concerned for the state of his country. "Democracy and freedom of expression in South Korea are at a real low point right now. We've become a society that doesn't tolerate dissent," he said.

Choi spent the first 26 years of his →

89
INDEXONCENSORSHIP.ORG

RIGHT:
Choi Seung-ho
questions a
National
Intelligence Service
official outside a
Seoul courtroom

→ career riding high as a reporter for MBC, a major public broadcaster. By doggedly digging into some of the darkest stories in his country, he is regarded as a swashbuckling hero by some and a dangerous troublemaker by others.

As a journalist, Choi is drawn to big stories of institutional malfeasance, and relishes holding powerful figures' feet to the fire. He has taken on South Korea's most heralded scientist, the wealthy elite who stash their money in overseas accounts, and a sitting president, Lee Myung-bak, who invested millions of dollars of public money in an ill-fated ecological project.

Choi's run as a television anchor ended in 2012, when, along with other journalists, he was dismissed for participating in a strike undertaken by two public broadcasters. The journalists argued that since the report on President Lee's failed ecological project, the network's president, who was appointed directly by Lee, had interfered in editorial matters and prohibited any coverage critical of Lee's administration.

When the strike was deemed illegal, Choi's job was terminated. Not one to miss a beat, he teamed up with other dismissed

Being wholly independent now is stressful, because it means I don't have the stable support of a big company

journalists to found Newstapa, a viewer-supported online news site that specialises in stories on the misdeeds of South Korea's government and big business.

Choi thinks it is noteworthy that years ago he was able to do investigative reporting for a major broadcaster, and have it run on national television during primetime, but nowadays he has to rely on

crowdfunding to make his work possible, and he has to show it in cinemas. "No one today would get permission to do what I was able to do then. It shows how far the situation has deteriorated," he said.

He argues that there is an urgent need for the kind of dogged reporting he does. "Being wholly independent now is stressful, because it means I don't have the stable support of a big company, but it frees me to report on whatever I want. I don't have to worry about possibly annoying any bosses or advertisers."

Beyond the strong response to Spy Nation, Choi has one more reason for optimism: next year South Koreans go to polls to elect a new president. He hopes for an end to a decade of right-wing rule, that freedom of expression will be higher on the electoral agenda, and that his work may help this come about.

Choi's work is openly opinionated, and he isn't shy about expressing his opinion that the South Korean government ought to change its ways and end its repressive tactics. "As a journalist, all you can really do is tell a story truthfully, and hope the public responds and creates some kind of pressure for reform," he said. ⊗

Steven Borowiec is based in Seoul, South Korea, and a regular contributor to Index on Censorship magazine

CREDIT: Newstapa

FRONTLINE CLUB London

"Frontline will be remembered as one of the high peaks of journalism. Martha Gellhorn certainly thought so, and she was a pretty good judge."
— John Simpson

Through its extensive programme of debates, screenings and workshops, the Frontline Club promotes engagement and dialogue on international affairs, champions independent journalism and provides a diverse range of training for journalists and other media workers. While the restaurant serves classic, elegant British food.

The Frontline Club
13 Norfolk Place, Paddington, London W2 1QJ
www.frontlineclub.com

Frontline Club Events and Workshops
+44 (0)20 7479 8940

Frontline Restaurant
+44 (0)20 7479 8960

MERCANTILE
CULTURE

CULTURE

IN THIS SECTION

PICTURED: A Pataxo tribesman in Brasilia demonstrating against the destruction of
his ancestral lands in the Amazon

Credit: Ueslei Marcelino/Reuters

Back from the Amazon

45(04): 94/99 I DOI: 10.1177/0306422016685997

Brazilian novelist and poet **Paulo Scott** doesn't believe writers have an obligation to anyone but, as he tells **Kieran Etoria-King**, he often finds himself confronting political and social issues

AFTER LIONEL SHRIVER'S speech at the Brisbane Writers' Festival, in which she ridiculed the argument that it is wrong for a white author to attempt to write about a culture which is not their own, there has been much debate in literary circles about who is allowed to write certain stories.

Try suggesting to novelist and poet Paulo Scott though, that Nowhere People, his novel about the struggle of a young indigenous girl from the Amazon, was a story he shouldn't have told, and you'll receive a good-natured scoff. The light-skinned author, who claims a book of poems he wrote about the invisibility of dark-skinned Brazilians is his least discussed work, is happy to speak for the unheard.

"I know that a few leaders read the book and thought that it was a very important contribution to their fight," he said of the response to Nowhere People. "If you talk with the indigenous leaders, they will say to you that the war they started to fight centuries ago is still on, because the annihilation and holocaust is still happening."

Musing on the issue of his own ethnicity, he said: "It's crazy but I am considered white, but my father is black, my younger brother is black – real dark-skinned. The main issues here in Brazil are connected with this necessity to find an identity, and it's necessary to talk about these unequal situations." He says these issues always influence his thinking when choosing things to write about, and he has often given up on projects because he was "too inside the political view".

When he does find that subtlety, though, he always has something to say. "Maybe my poetry isn't quite deep or quite original. When you see the poetry from all over the world, you can say that I'm not the best poet, but still I have my strange voice," he said.

That voice is tangible in the poems published below by Index on Censorship, translated into English for the first time from his acclaimed collection Mesmo sem →

RIGHT: Novelist and poet Paulo Scott

→ dinheiro comprei um esqueite novo (Even Without Money I Bought a New Skateboard).

Here, Scott looks inwards, examining his own life, but he also takes aim more broadly at the listlessness of his country. His generation, the generation which fought against Brazil's military dictatorship, has failed spectacularly in Scott's eyes, despite all it promised. He wants Brazilians to stop looking for some "other" they can blame, and take responsibility for the future.

"Here in Brazil we want to be Americans, we want to be part of the 'American way', and sometimes we are blind, we can't see what we are. I'm talking about myself but also about my generation, about the difficulty to find a way out of your situation, and about the difference between fiction and reality," he said. ⊗

Kieran Etoria-King is an editorial assistant at Index on Censorship magazine

Perhaps in a letter

the convenience
of just being someone strange
with strange ideas
isn't enough any more

you wanted to with all your strength
and now you've turned into a kind of
unbreakable monster

and the camera that was
accompanying you doesn't exist any more
and all you think about is
how to get by

the dream others envy
is nothing but the only way
to get out of bed before the clock
in the kitchen strikes noon

beginners make up that they drank
with you and stayed up all night
with you and got up to all sorts
in bed with you – all lies

so in a party with free whisky
a cute girl with short hair
comes up close to you
and says she feels sorry for you

says you're becoming
as pathetic as the characters
you invented

what'll be left of everything? literature?
what the hell's the point of literature
when you're happy and in love?
(to love is something that's never completed)

I've got to write down that
never is a person too old
I need to get back on form

we're hypnotised
wanting to be djs and radio-show hosts
playwrights and film-makers

we should be a source of hope
– what a ridiculous generation
that swore never to promise
what it couldn't deliver

the birds sing at
six in the morning
here in rio de janeiro –
you alone are responsible

throw out the shortcuts
try not to blame anyone else

Adverbs

the poet is expected to wash his hands
before and after using the urinal
and not to get distracted by the temporary disrepair
(or even the malformation) of the tiles
on the bathroom wall if there are
tiles on the bathroom wall and someone
waiting at the table

the poet is expected to be stone
and, being stone, to wait at the table until the others
tire of the team game that solitude is
until (being invariably stone)
he really is stone and someone unaware
comes to clean him with water, disinfectant and scouring pad

→

and sets up à la IKEA a barbecue grill
that possibly will never be used
the poet is expected to be decisive
but not necessarily good-looking
and to like pets and children
and a fair settling of accounts and surfing in Santa Catarina

and being of stone (and a godfather) to remember to send
birthday cards, trying never
to be reckless when talking about the future or love
because in the universe of collections of stones
nothing's more cheesy than a letter that's hurried
but still a love letter

The medal girl

the medal girl is the girl with the medals
earns her living presenting medals
in swimming competitions

it's a job like any other
and could be good fun if the other girls
were the kind to have a laugh

the athletes don't have a laugh
because they're focused and need to win
not every athlete appreciates the medal girls

being the medal girl is just one of the jobs
of our medal girl – this month
she'll also be a hostess at a party

a party in the early hours of Christmas Day
she'll earn almost ten times more than she earns
as the medal girl, but she won't have time

time to sit and chat – the medal girl
had eight different jobs this year
and the year's not over

the medal girl will earn a red dress
for working at the party – to be part
of a moment of victory is to be part

of a moment of beauty

the medal girl is evidence of beauty
and of luck – beauty isn't luck or intelligence
an athlete needs to be intelligent

the medal girl has family, but they're not from here
the medal girl woke up – beauty, the dress, the party
the medal girl makes an effort: our medal girl

beauty is a present

Rubber

come, hide your feet
slip them into this water
it'll still be good for
me to wash in

everything's perfect
but carry on, go on –
possibly hostile
to what's left

pretending not to know
that I can be sad
but I can't be sad
by your side

Translated by **Stefan Tobler**

Paulo Scott *is a novelist and poet. A former lawyer and activist, he taught law at university for 10 years before moving to Rio de Janeiro in 2008 to become a full-time writer. He has published four books of poetry and four works of fiction*

A story from the disappeared

45(04): 100/106 | DOI: 10.1177/0306422016685998

Four decades after **Haroldo Conti** was arrested, one of the award-winning Argentine writer's short stories is published for the first time in English. **Jon Lindsay Miles** looks back at his career

JUST BEFORE HE was murdered 40 years ago, Argentine writer Haroldo Conti was warned that his life was in danger. This was at the start of a military dictatorship that led to right-wing death squads killing thousands. Conti, then 51, was likely to have been on the authorities' radar, because of his success. He had won the Casa de las Américas Prize for his novel Mascaró el cazador americano (Mascaró, The American Hunter) the previous year, and he had been offering his home in Buenos Aires as a place of refuge for other writers under threat of kidnap and murder.

Conti decided against exile, but in the early hours of 5 May 1976, he was arrested at his apartment. Later a witness described him under detention in a police barracks, in a pitiful condition, incontinent and unable to talk or eat, having been severely tortured.

Conti's novels and stories cannot be called political if this is taken to mean that their principal subject matter is a depiction of political activity, nor in the sense of arguing for writing as a militant act, but there are later stories which quietly reflect the effect of the author's two visits to Cuba in the early 1970s to sit on the jury of the literary prize he later won.

The participation of ordinary folk in the formal institutions of Cuban society much impressed Conti, and he publicly announced himself a politically committed writer after his second visit to the island. He decided in his next major work to take on a grander theme: America – stretching in the Hispanic mind from Alaska to Tierra del Fuego. This became the subject matter of Mascaró.

RIGHT: Author Haroldo Conti who vanished after he was taken into police custody

OPPOSITE: The Haroldo Conti Museum on the Tigre delta. The little wooden house where Conti would go to write is as he left it, with a desk beside the river. Many visitors still come to see where the author worked

His final novel avoided direct political references in its description of a travelling circus, but Conti's prologue might be taken to indicate an allegorical relationship with events in his homeland, referring as it does to "this land of struggle and hope called America".

Certainly the censors took exception to Mascaró after its publication: despite acknowledging the absence in it of any directly declared political position, the censors' report draws the conclusion that Conti's novel "fosters the diffusion of ideologies, doctrines or political, economic or social systems that are Marxist, intending to abolish the principles held by our National Constitution".

But Conti's political instinct was principally an expression of his interest in ordinary folk: in men as individuals, not man in the abstract. In an interview with writer Rodolfo Benasso in 1969, Conti argued against "the pretension of a novel that embraces and exhausts once and for all some supposed national reality".

In the story Muerte de un hermano,

The participation of ordinary folk in the formal institutions of Cuban society much impressed Conti

published for the first time in English, overleaf, as A Brother's Death, we meet one of the many solitary men who wander through Conti's work, characters enriched by the author's own experience of countless hours spent in the company of ordinary men.

"Between literature and life," he said to Benasso, "I choose life"; and here Conti breathes the richness of a human life even into the story of a death. ⊗

Haroldo Conti was a writer, screenwriter and teacher. He remains on the list of persons who disappeared during Argentina's dictatorship (1976 to 1983)

Jon Lindsay Miles is a writer and translator working in Spain. He is currently preparing a translation of Haroldo Conti's novel In Life for a 2018 release →

A Brother's Death

To my mother

He didn't even feel the blow. The old chap only felt a tender numbness climbing from his feet. Several voices rose towards the middle of the street, and after that they gently moved away.

The man came close, emerging from the mist that was around him, and bent his body over him.

"Juan ..."

The man sent out a smile.

"Juan!"

"How are you, brother?"

"Where did you come from, Juan?"

He pointed down towards him with the smile still on his face.

"Didn't I tell you I'd be back one day?"

"Yes ... That's what you said ... Of course!"

The mist began to fluctuate behind the figure's shoulder. There were stick-like shadows coming close, but when he tried to make out who they were they compressed, before drawing into a hem that formed a circle all around him.

"Juan, my little brother ..."

He moved his head from side to side.

"So much time has passed ... You've no idea how long it's been ..."

"I know."

"No, no you don't! ... Because for you the time is something else. I'm talking about my time, lad ... I waited for you, sure I did ... I said to all these people," and he tried to raise his hand to them, "these people ..."

His eyes drew narrow and he looked at him determinedly. No doubt that it was him. It was the same face, hard and honest.

"I had my doubts as well, you know," he nodded, speaking low.

And his voice broke in his throat.

"Well, it's understandable."

"I suppose it is at that ..."

"Deep down you knew I'd come, though. Isn't that the truth, my brother?"

He pointed at him once again; an old flame rose inside him.

"Of course! Yes of course!"

He tried to raise his body and to hug the little brother who had finally returned, but found his legs would not allow him to. He couldn't even feel them, now. He let his body go on to the surface of the road, with just his hands to hold him up, to keep that lovely face in view.

"And how did you get on there, lad?" he asked him with a smile.

||||||||||||||||||||||||||||||||||||||||||||||||||||||||||||||||||||||||||||||||||||||||||||||||

FROM THE ARCHIVE

TAKEN AND KILLED

Haroldo Conti's disappearance was first reported in the September 1976 edition of Index on Censorship magazine which recounted how military police forced their way into his home, beat him up and dragged him into a waiting car. Index described his abduction as an attempt by the Argentine military government to create an "atmosphere of terror." In 1981, celebrated Colombian author Gabriel Garcia Marquez confirmed in an article for Index journalists had been told of Conti's death. He recalled how his friend had been reluctant to leave his home country despite receiving many threats. Marquez described Conti as one of Argentina's greatest writers, and as a man who was "never ashamed of his great love for life".

Both articles can be found in the Index archive: ***ioc.sagepub.com***

He tried to seem quite natural. In truth he felt much better than he had done in a long time, the old body wasn't heavy now, it didn't weigh a thing.

"Fine ... Fine."

"Honestly! This Juan! ... Is that all you've got to say?"

"I never was a chatterbox."

"No, you never were ... Barely said more than the old man ... Only two or three words more."

He smiled then at the memory of their father and of Juan, that old Juan quite like this one. Perhaps the same completely.

"Your singing was spot on, though. Do you still keep up that lovely voice?"

"Yes, I think I do."

"And do you sing as well?"

"Still. A man who goes alone like me, he's always singing something."

"Many people are alone here too, if this is what you're saying, but they hardly ever sing."

At this he paused because a feeling of great weariness came over him.

"I thought of you at times and sang. In truth it was the only way I found I could remember."

He lowered his head towards the road and added in a murmur:

"Nobody looks kindly on an old man who just sings because ... I did my best to tell them ... tried ... but you know how these people are. They come and go all day ... I think the corporal understood me once. He smiled at me at least, and said: Go on, old chap. Sing it again."

He lifted up his head once more.

"Juan, my little brother, I have also walked a long way."

→

→ And a thick tear rolled right down his cheek.

Juan reached his hand out silently and patted him softly, though the hand was broad and powerful.

"I didn't think you'd come, now. That's the truth of it. Forgive me, but it's what I came to think."

"What does it matter now? I've come, and now I'm going to take you."

"That's exactly what I said, Juan! Say it again now, Juan, I want the world to hear you say it!"

"That's right …"

"He'll come, I always said, one day my big brother Juan will come, and then we'll be together … What is it, Juan? Juan!"

"I'm here, lad. Don't you worry."

"I thought you'd gone."

"No need to worry."

He reached and put his hand back on his shoulder once again.

This was how Juan was. You didn't have to spell things out for him. He understood and took it in. Everything. At once. The big hand on his shoulder sent a current through him somehow. He was something like a tree that has its roots firm in the ground and all the sounds of earth within it, and it holds the birds and skies as well.

Many years ago and with this same hand on his shoulder, he had said almost these very words. "Don't worry. I'll come back for you. One day I'll come back." They had been walking on the dirt road where the countryside begins; it was the morning of an autumn day. Juan had wanted no one else but him to go along. They'd walked in silence through the country and he hadn't looked back even once. And then they'd come out on the road – the morning had now dawned – and when the car came into view he'd put his hand on to his shoulder and he'd said that line of words. And then he'd disappeared around a bend.

He'd asked himself, and more than once, where the thought had come from. He was a man who worked the land, just like their father did before him. Perhaps it was the road close by, that stripe of greyish-brown that came and went at the horizon and on which from time to time a sleepy car would roll along, or else the smaller, slower figure of some wanderer who raised his hand to send a nod towards them before he vanished in the bend with all the road for him alone, from one end to the other, and the road you couldn't see as well: the world, in other words.

There was in him, in any case, something not in others. In that hard and trusting face there was some mark or sign that lit up when he looked along the road, or when he simply used to mention it. And then one day Juan started out.

Some time after that, the road had taken off their mother in a carriage made for sorrows.

And then there came the difficult years. The land turned hard and sullen and their father became curt and gruff. He went off in the same hearse as the one that took their mother in the winter of '37.

Until one August morning he had gone out on the road as well, and waited for the car and gone. The house had vanished round the bend and disappeared, for ever.

Most of life came after this, but made up of a line of years which hadn't left him memories, and scarcely any year that was more wretched than another. Ten years poor and miserable. Poverty and hard times and the oldness of the city.

Perhaps in truth he'd been a little pleased to feel this poverty, once he had accepted it. No one understands this. But he was happy at the end of things, or almost, in his way. The only thing to worry about was being at the hostel door at six o'clock each evening to make sure no tramp would pinch the bed that stood beside the window. The white, enormous buildings seen from here and at this hour appeared to float there in the kindly light. And then they slowly darkened. Then the lights would roam the night at heights that left one feeling puzzled, and the city disappeared somehow, and he thought about the distant house, the country, young and ample.

Then he saw the road again and heard the words Juan said to him. He didn't always manage to remember Juan completely as for this he needed help from things belonging more to those days, like the songs and gleaming signals. His brother had grown inside him, though, was something more alive than him regardless of his absence. There was a time and place, precisely when the old folk and the vagrants came to gather at the hostel where they →

→ waited for the doors to open. Then, and who knows why it was, but Juan was wholly there, or he was very nearly whole and in the midst of this misfortune. And this at least propelled him to the bed next to the window.

Except the image had grown paler lately, even not appeared some days. And if he got the bed then this was not due to his brother but because there wasn't anyone now who wanted to compete for it.

In truth, it was some time now since the matter had stopped interesting him. No more nor less than that. The years had brought him down at last. Inside he was dried up and now consented to be blown round like an old, discarded shell.

He looked at Juan and tried to smile.

"Things blow you back and forward like an old, discarded shell. Just that ..."

"What is it you're telling me?"

"I'm wondering how it happened, all this."

"Why is that important, lad?"

"It isn't, of course, at all. I'm only saying that things happened without any help from me."

His voice was tamed and hurting.

"Yes, but that's the way things are."

"Not for you, not you my lad ... You leaped onto life and then you tamed it like you'd tame a colt. Isn't that the truth, Juan?"

"No, it wasn't like that. Well, I can't say how it really was. The thing is that I never stop to ask myself these questions ... I take things as they come to me."

"That's it, lad. That's right. You closed your hand into a fist and shoved it deep into your pocket! Juan, are you still there, Juan?"

The figure seemed to drift and sway.

"I'm here."

"Please could you take my hand?"

"Of course!"

His face had almost gone, now. But he felt the hard and roughened hand.

He didn't know what time it was, but even so this silence in a city street seemed strange.

"What's happened to all the people?"

He had asked himself the question without really being curious, as he fought to hold his head up when it seemed to be escaping him.

"It must be very late."

The figure swayed towards him now, and with his final thread of voice he said, still:

"Are we going, Juan?"

The voice he heard was very close to him.

"When you want, my lad."

"Then, now ..."

Poems for Kim

||||||||||||||||||||||||||||||||||||||||||||||||||

45(04): 107/109 I DOI: 10.1177/0306422016685999

Jang Jin-sung was the North Korean regime's favourite poet – until he defected to the South. **Sybil Jones** speaks to him about his past life as a propagandist

"I COULD ONLY BE inspired to write poems that manifested my devotion to the leader," said Jang Jin-sung of his time working as a state poet in North Korea.

Before his defection in 2004, Jang Jin-sung – a pseudonym – was a favoured poet of the dictator Kim Jong-il. He was employed as a psychological warfare officer in the ruling Workers' Party of Korea's clandestine United Front Department, writing pro-North propaganda, in his case as poems, for distribution in the South.

Jang's job was not just one of literary talents, but also one of extraordinary trust and risk. For his poems to be credible, they had to seem as if they were written by South Koreans, which meant incorporating the subtly different southern colloquialisms and cultural allusions. To do so, he was given special permission to immerse himself in the UFD's library of South Korean books, films and TV programmes. Accessing such proscribed tomes would normally mean instant incarceration – if not execution – for ordinary North Koreans.

The state's National Board of Arts regulated the language of all poetry, but Jang's verses were met with approval and he was rewarded with a comfortable lifestyle in Pyongyang. But this was in the 1990s, when the country could no longer feed its citizens, who died in huge numbers. Jang's realisation that the state was using propaganda to keep power while its citizens died en masse ultimately led him to undertake a dangerous and dramatic escape to China, and thence to South Korea. He recounted the journey in his 2014 memoir Dear Leader.

Today, North Korea is still infamous for its opacity, its lack of a free press and free speech, and its isolation from the world's media. It consistently ranks near the bottom of the free press indexes. However, there is much reportage about the country that is based on rumour and speculation. In 2011 Jang moved to counter that. He set up →

ABOVE: Poet Jang Jin-sung in front of the Gwanghwamun gate in downtown Seoul

ABOVE: A North Korean propaganda poster from 2009 glorifying the country's armed forces

Credit: akg-images / Pictures From History

→ New Focus International, a news website that publishes analyses, first-hand insights and almost real-time news from networks of North Koreans both in and out of the country, while organising conferences and advising governments on North Korea.

He told Index: "Restrictions on nationalisms, inspiration, and language do not exist in the free world I live in now." But he lamented: "I keep telling myself inwardly: 'I mustn't be happy.' I feel guilty that I live a better life than the people I left behind in North Korea. That

must explain why the main subjects, and who I wrote for in my poetry, are North Korea and its people." The first three new poems, below, about life in North Korea, were written exclusively for Index by Jang. The fourth poem, Ode to the Smiling Sun, was written by Jang when he was still working in North Korea. Smiling Sun was the name given to former Supreme Leader Kim Il-sung after his death in 1994.

It drew controversy for associating "tears" and sadness with Kim Il-sung. Jang justified this as a new tactic to show the leader's sacrifice for his people; how he had suppressed his own tears and continually smiled for the good of the nation. In Dear Leader Jang recalled how a colleague had reminded Jang that a former state poet had once employed the word "dew" to refer euphemistically to the leader's tears and was "banished to the countryside for 10 years". ⊗

Jang Jin-sung lives in South Korea. His memoir *Dear Leader was published in 2014*

Spoons

Perhaps it was because there was no rice,
That no spoons could be found in the house.
Even the spoons had been sold
To put food on the table of ancestral rites.

Just as all wish for happiness,
Drinking watery rice gruel
The family of five, in that house
Had a single wish
That if ever so slightly the burden of poverty could be eased
The family jewels could one day amount to
Not one spoon, but daresay
f
i
v
e

If it were rice

The child, who only knew grass-green gruel
Given white rice on their birthday,
Cried out and kicked in protest
Clinging to my heart, pleading, for rice.

Cold rice

How or where he had managed,
A dollop of cold rice
Was pushed back towards his wife
As the husband's kind voice reassured her -
I ate on the way.

Working in the fields all day,
Her in-laws returned from the mountains
A dollop of cold rice
Was pushed towards them, whilst feigning satiety -
This leftover rice is all we could offer.

Pregnant newcomer
Depriving her seemed like a sin incapable of atonement
That made the elderly couple's soul shrivel
They clasped their hands around it, like treasure -
This will last us till morning.

Even after that day
That cold rice went untouched.

Ode to the Smiling Sun

All the tears that were to have been shed by his people, our Supreme
Leader took on himself alone to shed. What smiles he had, he gave
them all so that his people might smile.
When the Supreme Leader gave the people his
gift of smiling, it manifested as his Love; when he sowed his gift on
our lands, it manifested as rays of the Sun; and as he left his gift for
history, it manifested as Immortal Life.

Index around the world

INDEX NEWS

45(04): 110/113 I DOI: 10.1177/0306422016686000

Protests, media monitoring and panel appearances were all part of Index's work over the past few months. **Kieran Etoria-King** takes a look at some of the events that stand out

ARRIVING OUTSIDE TURKEY'S embassy in London to protest Turkish President Erdogan's ongoing crackdown on free speech, Index on Censorship staff were told by the British policeman on guard to stand across the street because the Turkish ambassador might get "upset". We stood our ground: getting the ambassador's attention was partly what being there was all about.

So why organise a protest? "It reminds the people who are behind bars that somebody outside is still rooting for them," said Index CEO Jodie Ginsberg. "It gives them a sense of hope, it gives them a sense that the fight is not lost, and it's important also to show the authorities that these individuals haven't been forgotten, because detention is a way to try and hide individuals away. Governments don't want their crimes and human rights violations known about. Making a noise, at least in some small symbolic way, helps remind governments that the people they've imprisoned and ideas they are seeking to suppress haven't been."

RIGHT: Editor of Index on Censorship magazine, Rachael Jolley (centre), chairs a panel at London's Frontline Club on the difficulties of reporting from warzones

It was with the intention of drawing attention to those behind bars that Ginsberg wrote to Prince Charles ahead of his official visit to Bahrain in November. As a significant trading partner with Bahrain, she believes that Britain has a responsibility to condemn the nation's treatment of people such as Nabeel Rajab, the activist and Index Freedom of Expression award winner who has seen his sentencing repeatedly delayed after being imprisoned for comments on Twitter. At the time of going to print, Rajab's trial was set for 15 December.

"If he [Prince Charles] is going to go there, then he needs to go with as much information as possible," Ginsberg said of her offer to brief the prince on Bahrain's human rights situation.

As part of its other advocacy and media monitoring work, Mapping Media Freedom project officer Hannah Machlin flew to Moscow in September. She spoke at the On The Tightrope conference, debating the future of journalism in a fragmenting Europe. Machlin met with representatives from most of the independent national media outlets in Russia.

"It was incredibly inspiring to meet with people doing great journalism despite the fact that they are operating in a near-complete climate of fear," she said.

"I spoke to a journalist who told me that after pieces are published she is always looking over her shoulder because she feels paranoid. Another said that he just assumes he is under more or less constant surveillance from the state. Unfortunately, it's just part of being an independent journalist in Russia."

In the past few months, the MMF team, who oversee crowdsourced reports of media harassment from around Europe, have been inundated by reports from Turkey, as the post-coup crackdown on journalists and government critics continued. MMF received 124 reports on Turkey from 1 July to 1 November, including reporting on the closure

He is under more or less constant surveillance from the state. Unfortunately, it's just part of being an independent journalist in Russia

of 15 pro-Kurdish media organisations and 13 journalists from Cumhuriyet newspaper being detained on terror charges. Machlin said: "Violations to press freedom in Turkey have consistently risen and press freedom has severely deteriorated in 2016."

What a Liberty!, Index's youth project, launched to reimagine the Magna Carta for the 21st Century, has grown into a movement of its own. The group's members have now taken over management of the project, with a year-long campaign plan to encourage young people to take part in further discussions and film showings. In late September, three of the group – Darshan Leslie, Ché Applewhaite and Mohamed Adan – attended the British Film Institute's Flip the Script, a day where young filmmakers and artists →

ABOVE:
Photographer Paul Conroy talks about the future role of foreign correspondents at the Frontline Club

Searching for a wi-fi connection can expose users to invasions of privacy and endanger journalists in the field

ABOVE:
Technology writer Cory Doctorow explains the challenges of anonymity at the launch of the autumn edition of Index on Censorship magazine

→ were urged to talk about how they wanted to see their generation portrayed in the media. The three What a Liberty! members hosted a panel discussion, alongside Index head of advocacy Melody Patry, where they talked about the importance of open debate, and examined the merit of limits meant to protect people from offensive speech. "It's really exciting to see how What a Liberty! has expanded," Leslie said. "This will inform how we go forward because we'll be able to draw from those messages about speaking up

and making sure you have a voice and using it properly." To find out more about What a Liberty! visit www.whataliberty.co.uk.

Index's youth advisory board, a selected group of young people from around the world who advise and inform Index's work, continued to meet every month via Google Hangout to discuss freedom of expression.

The board shot and published videos drawing attention to murdered media workers around the world, in support of International Day to End Impunity for Crimes Against Journalists. The day, part of IFEX's No Impunity campaign, was held to demand action against the alarming rate of attacks on journalists that go unsolved, or are not even investigated, all over the world – according to IFEX research, nine out of 10 cases since 2006 remain unpunished.

CREDIT: (left) Sean Gallagher; (right) Sean Gallagher

The autumn issue of the magazine was launched with an event held at the office of the VPN software company Hide My Ass, to discuss the value of anonymity. Technology journalist Geoff White mined data from every smartphone in the room to demonstrate how simple actions such as searching for a wi-fi connection can expose users to invasions of privacy and endanger journalists in the field. He told Index: "What troubles me is that, talking to journalists, there's this idea of, 'I've survived Baghdad, I've survived here, I've survived there, what have I got to fear from my phone?' But it can give away such valuable information – location data and who you're meeting." In the second half of the session Canadian writer Cory Doctorow discussed the long struggle to make people care about protecting their personal information online.

Index has also started the initial stages of the judging process for the 2017 Freedom of Expression Awards. The short list will be announced on 17 January 2017. Last year's award winner Smockey, the rapper who led a revolution in Burkina Faso, is raising funds to rebuild his music studio after it was burned down for the second time in a year. He played a concert at Ouagadougou's Revolution Square on 15 October to mark the two-year anniversary of the country's successful uprising against former president Blaise Compaoré. He called on those implicated in crimes by the previous government to face trial, telling Index: "Burkina Faso literally means 'the land of men with integrity', so we would like to trust the justice of our country."

Staff have taken part in many events around the world over the past few months. Index on Censorship magazine editor Rachael Jolley chaired a panel at London's Frontline Club on the future challenges for foreign correspondents and difficulties of reporting from warzones. Ginsberg was a panellist at a debate at October's Battle of Ideas festival at London's Barbican,

called Comedy and Censorship: Are You Kidding Me?, where she argued for comedians' right to be offensive. Citing Scottish stand-up Frankie Boyle and Australian Jim Jefferies as her favourite examples of comedians who sometimes cause outrage, she said: "Jefferies' stuff on gun law in the United States is just brilliant, and shocking, and I

You do sometimes need to shock because otherwise how do we get shaken out of our complacencies

think sometimes in order to have the truth stuck in our faces, you do sometimes need to shock, because otherwise how do we get shaken out of complacencies?" ⊗

Kieran Etoria-King is the Liverpool John Moores/Tim Hetherington fellow for 2016. He is the editorial assistant at Index on Censorship

BELOW: Two audience members check out the anonymity masks at the launch of the autumn issue of Index on Censorship magazine

Where's our president?

END NOTE ||||||||||||||||||||||||||||||||||||||||||||||||||||||||||||||||||||||||||

45(04): 114/116 | DOI: 10.1177/0306422016686001

When their president went missing, Malawians used a humorous hashtag to force his return. **Kiri Kankhwende** examines how the power of social media is helping to increase pressure for transparency

"**HOW DOES A** whole president go missing? How?" "Malawians understand why their president would rather be in America. But they're saying 'come & let's suffer together'."

These tongue-in-cheek posts on Twitter and Facebook began after Malawi's president, Peter Mutharika, failed to return from the 71st UN General Assembly, which ended on 26 September 2016. The president and his entourage had left the country on 15 September but as weeks passed and the government refused to elaborate on what exactly the president was still doing in the USA – journalists were told he was running the country via Skype – citizens and reporters used the hashtag #BringBackMutharika to draw international media attention to his unexplained absence and to press for transparency from his administration.

When the president finally returned to Malawi from the USA a month later, on 16 October, apparently healthy, it remained unclear why he had disappeared. But the ability to mount the social media campaign to get Mutharika back and openly challenge Malawi's system of government is a sign that the country has come some way since the days of Hastings Kamuzu Banda's 30-year virtual dictatorship.

A riff on the #BringBackOurGirls hashtag used in Nigeria, #BringBackMutharika put the government on the back foot, exposing shortcomings in its PR operation and revealing an arrogant mindset more suited to the era before the advent of multi-party democracy in Malawi, a time when the government would not have had to explain itself. In a commentary, Nyasa Times, a privately owned media outlet, pointed out that the confusion reaffirmed "the fact that we have a system whose one foot is in autocracy and another in democracy."

Among the funny memes and mocking "missing president" posters on the hashtag, there were tones of frustration and concern. Rumours abounded that the 76-year-old president was in hospital. They were able to gain traction because the last time a Malawian president's whereabouts were unknown and the state house was obfuscating, he actually was dead.

Peter Mutharika's brother, Bingu Mutharika, died in office in 2012, but the state house deliberately misled the press and public for two days while efforts were made for an extra-constitutional

arrangement for his succession. Eventually, however, the constitution was upheld and the then vice president Joyce Banda assumed the office before her defeat to Peter Mutharika in the 2014 elections.

The trust lost by the government in the eyes of the public during those tense couple of days has not yet been restored and #BringBackMutharika was about more than an unexplained absence; it was also about accountability and governance at a time when people are facing considerable hardship. Malawians face a dire economic situation characterised by poor basic service provision in areas such as housing and education, and exacerbated by regular electricity blackouts and severe water

#BringBackMutharika was about more than an unexplained absence

shortages. Opposition politicians put the cost for the president's US trip at an estimated $1.7 million.

Malawi's independent media has given voice to people's frustrations, drawing parallels between the government press office's lies in 2012 and its ongoing resistance to transparency. The press releases from the government about the president's mysterious absence betrayed irritation at being forced to explain the president's whereabouts, condemning →

ABOVE: Malawi's president Peter Mutharika of the Democratic Progressive Party waves to supporters in Blantyre

→ the social media activism and warning journalists and the public against speculating about the president's health.

When he finally returned to Malawi from the USA, a journalist from the Zodiak Broadcasting Station, an independent media outlet, was arrested while filming the motorcade. His arrest and those of human rights activists staging peaceful protests against the water and electricity crisis in the

The press have shown they are increasingly emboldened to hold the government to account

country were condemned in a joint statement by civil society organisations The Centre for Human Rights and Rehabilitation and Centre for Development of People, which urged the government "to stop rolling back the gains made in media freedom in the country."

The situation for privately owned

BELOW: Author Kiri Kankhwende

independent media in Malawi has become increasingly embattled. In 2010 and 2011, the late President Bingu Mutharika drew international condemnation for his increasingly illiberal actions towards the press, including the intimidation and arrests of journalists who criticised his administration, the introduction of legislation to restrict press freedom and threats to close down privately owned media houses. Reporters Without Borders had noted an improvement in press freedom in Malawi when he was first elected but voiced concern in later years. Under his brother, although the country improved its ranking from 73rd in the world for press freedom to 59th in 2015, the country has slid back down the scale this year, to 66th place.

The figures are instructive but what they do not portray is the creeping chill of government intimidation, which is felt in press conferences that are sometimes packed with the president's supporters, who create a scene more akin to a political rally. The press conference after Mutharika's return from the USA was no different and journalists claimed harassment.

It was issues such as this which prompted privately owned media houses and press freedom organisations to issue the Mount Soche Declaration on 8 November, in which they threatened to boycott government press conferences unless press freedom is guaranteed. They also pledged to seek legal redress for violations of the constitutional right to freedom of the press.

Malawi's young democracy has withstood some crucial tests since 1994, while the press have shown that they are increasingly emboldened to hold the government to account. As the #BringBackMutharika episode shows, Malawians want answers from their government. ⊗

Kiri Kankhwende is a Malawian journalist and blogger based in London. She tweets @madomasi

CREDIT: Wasi Danju